Major 1980
Tax Cut Proposals

DATE DUE

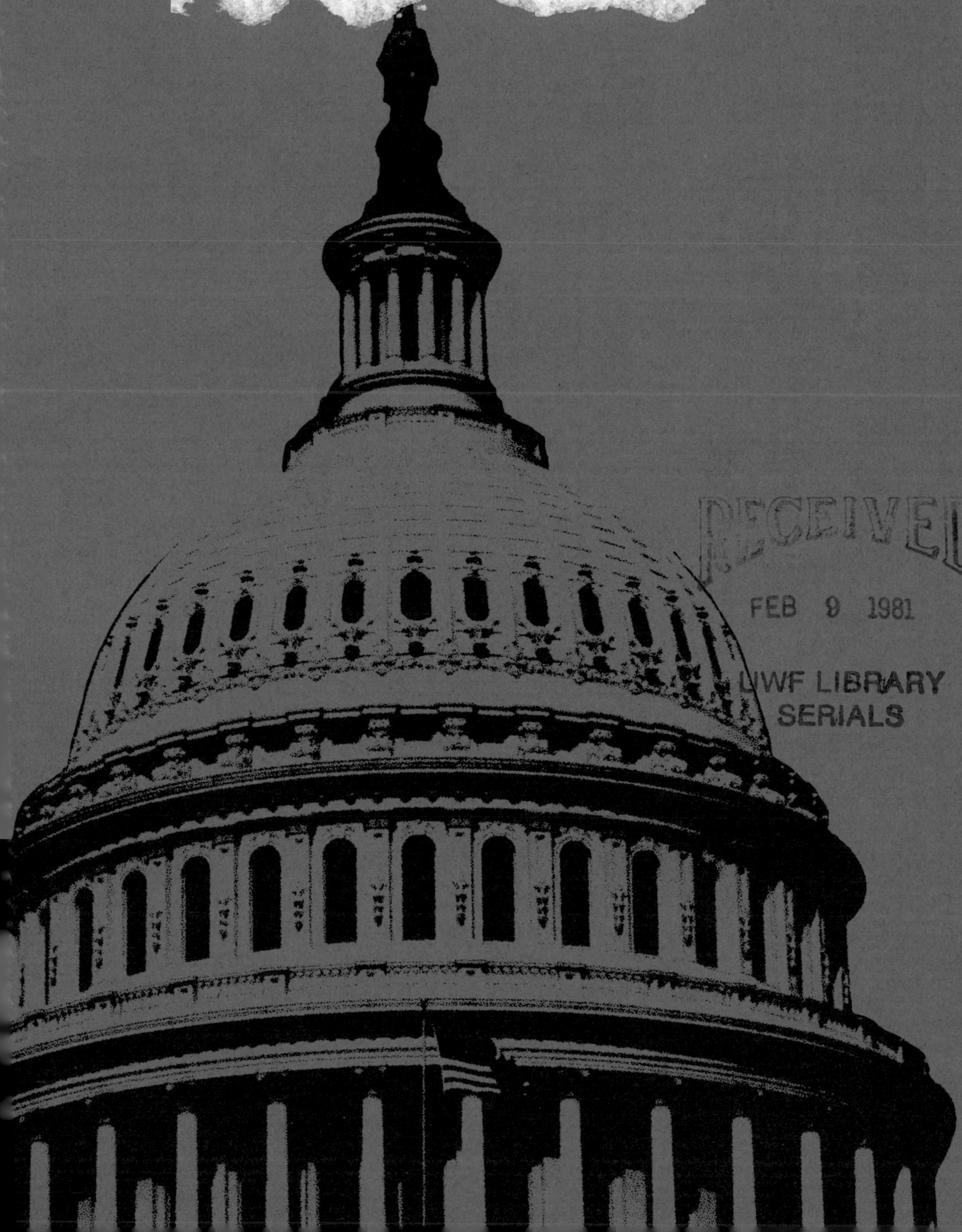

AEI LEGISLATIVE ANALYSES

Balanced analyses of current proposals before the Congress, prepared with the help of specialists in law, economics, and government

Major 1980 Tax Cut Proposals

1980

96th Congress

2nd Session

AMERICAN ENTERPRISE INSTITUTE

for Public Policy Research

Washington and London

ISBN-0-8447-0236-6
Legislative Analysis No. 21, 96th Congress
December 1980

CONTENTS

Tables

1

INTRODUCTION

Governor Ronald Reagan and numerous Republican members of the Congress announced on June 24, 1980, a proposed major federal income tax cut for adoption during the second session of the 96th Congress. The terms of this proposal were spelled out in bills introduced in the House of Representatives and Senate on June 25, 1980, as outlined in the section "The Republican Proposal." Senator Robert Dole (R-Kans.) offered this proposal to cut personal income taxes by an average of 10 percent and to establish a simplified system for the speedier depreciation of business assets as an amendment to the debt ceiling resolution (H. J. Res. 569) on June 26, 1980. This amendment was defeated in almost a straight party-line vote, and subsequent attempts to secure speedy adoption have not, as this analysis is written, succeeded. The president sharply attacked the Republican proposal and strongly recommended that consideration of a tax cut be postponed until after the November election. Announcement of the Republican tax cut plan, however, stimulated immediate action by Democratic members of the Senate Finance Committee to fashion an alternative tax cut plan. The administration did propose a number of tax law amendments in late August as part of its recommended economic revitalization program, but it declined to offer specific legislative language to implement its overall proposals until 1981. The Senate Finance Committee favorably reported its tax cut proposal early in September, and Governor Reagan promptly endorsed this plan as acceptable to him.

This analysis will examine the reasons for the wide agreement that taxes should be cut, the differences in opinion as to the cuts that should be made and their timing, the arguments advanced for and against the adoption of the three major tax cut proposals, and particular features of those proposals.

2

TAX CUT PROPOSALS

THE REPUBLICAN PROPOSAL

The "Tax Reduction–Job Creation Act" was introduced in the Senate by Senator Robert Dole (R-Kans.) and thirty-six other Republican senators as S. 2878 and in the House by Representative Barber B. Conable, Jr. (R-N.Y.) and eighteen co-sponsors as H.R. 7655. This bill would reduce marginal tax rates for individuals by an average of 10 percent in 1981. The marginal tax rate is the rate at which each extra dollar of income is taxed. This change would cut current tax rates of 14 to 70 percent to a range of 12 to 63 percent.[1] (See tables 1 and 2.)

The Republican proposal would also adopt the "Capital Cost Recovery Act" 10-5-3 accelerated depreciation plan to stimulate investment and to offset the effects of inflation on the tax treatment of business assets.[2] This proposal would simplify record keeping and tax compliance by reducing the 130 asset classes that are now employed for depreciation purposes to three classes.[3] This depreciation plan would allow buildings and structural components to be depreciated over a ten-year period, automobiles, taxis, and light-duty trucks over a three-year period, and all other qualifying assets, such as equipment and machinery over a five-year period. Ineligible property includes residential rental property, inventories, and land. These depreciation periods are, in general, much shorter than those allowed under current law. Shorter depreciation periods benefit businesses because the more rapidly depreciation is taken, the less its value is eroded by inflation. Accelerated depreciation, that is, the allowance of a higher percentage of an asset's value as depreciation in early years, is also beneficial to business even in a noninflationary environment as long as interest rates are above zero, since accelerated depreciation in effect provides an interest-free loan to the firm involved.[4]

The 10-5-3 depreciation system would be phased in over a five-year period by gradually reducing asset lives until they reached their new ones, although the plan would be effective for a few assets without a phase-in period. The plan would liberalize the investment tax credit somewhat—eligible structures and equipment would receive a 10 percent credit, and automobiles and trucks a 6 percent credit. Any gain from the sale of partially depreciated assets would be taxed as ordinary income. Salvage value would not be figured into an asset's depreciable base but would be taxed when realized on the sale of the asset. The Treasury could recover the investment tax credit taken on an asset if the asset is sold before it is fully depreciated. The 10-5-3 plan would depart significantly from the "useful life" concept for depreciating assets by assigning shorter, arbitrary asset lives for tax purposes. The real cost of investment would be reduced by this plan, and advocates expect that increased investment will boost economic growth and productivity with little effect on inflation.

2

TABLE 1

CURRENT MARGINAL TAX RATES FOR SINGLE TAXPAYERS AND THOSE SCHEDULED IN THE REPUBLICAN PROPOSAL

Taxable Income (in dollars)	Current Marginal Tax Rate (percentage of taxable income)	Proposed Marginal Tax Rate (percentage of taxable income)
Under 2,300	—	—
2,300–3,400	14	12
3,400–4,400	16	14
4,400–6,500	18	16
6,500–8,500	19	17
8,500–10,800	21	19
10,800–12,900	24	21
12,900–15,000	26	23
15,000–18,200	30	27
18,200–23,500	34	30
23,500–28,800	39	35
28,800–34,100	44	39
34,100–41,500	49	44
41,500–55,300	55	50
55,300–81,800	63	57
81,800–108,300	68	61
108,300 and over	70	63

SOURCE: Internal Revenue Service and S. 2878.

THE SENATE FINANCE COMMITTEE BILL

On August 21, 1980, the Senate Finance Committee announced its approval of a series of tax cut proposals that were added to a House-passed bill (H.R. 5829) by a vote of 11–1. Individual income tax rates would be reduced by one to three percentage points so that marginal tax rates for married couples would range from 12 to 67 percent instead of 14 to 70 percent, as at present. Some tax brackets would be narrowed in size. Individual taxpayers may claim an exemption of $1,000 and a like amount for each dependent under current law. Those who are over sixty-five and those who are blind are entitled to an additional exemption. The Senate proposal would raise the amount of this personal exemption to $1,100. The zero bracket amount (ZBA)—formerly the standard deduction—available to those who do not itemize their deductions establishes an amount of taxable income that is exempt from tax in lieu of itemized deductions. The ZBA currently stands at $2,300 for persons filing singly and $3,400 for persons filing jointly. The Senate bill would increase the ZBA to $2,400 and $3,600, respectively.

The earned income tax credit (EITC) was established in 1975 to ease the tax burden on low-income working families with dependent children and to increase work incentives for those receiving public assistance. Tax law currently allows an EITC equal to 10 percent of the first $5,000 of earned income for families with

3

TABLE 2

**CURRENT MARGINAL TAX RATES FOR MARRIED TAXPAYERS AND
THOSE SCHEDULED IN THE REPUBLICAN PROPOSAL**

Taxable Income (in dollars)	Current Marginal Tax Rate (percentage of taxable income)	Proposed Marginal Tax Rate (percentage of taxable income)
Under 3,400	—	—
3,400–5,500	14	12
5,500–7,600	16	14
7,600–11,900	18	16
11,900–16,000	21	19
16,000–20,200	24	22
20,200–24,600	28	25
24,600–29,900	32	28
29,900–35,200	37	33
35,200–45,800	43	39
45,800–60,000	49	44
60,000–85,600	54	49
85,600–109,400	59	53
109,400–162,400	64	58
162,400–215,400	68	61
215,400 and over	70	63

SOURCE: Internal Revenue Service and S. 2878.

dependent children, and the amount of the credit is phased out as earned income increases from $6,000 to $10,000. The Senate proposal would increase the credit to 11 percent and would raise the phase-out range to between $7,000 and $11,000. The committee proposed a new deduction that would be available to two-income couples who file a joint return to ameliorate the so-called marriage penalty imposed under the current system. This change would allow couples to deduct in 1981 an amount up to 5 percent of the first $30,000 of income of the spouse with lower earnings. This percentage would increase to 10 percent in 1982. It would be available whether or not the couple is subject to the marriage penalty.

Another change would allow Americans who are either residing in developing foreign nations (other than tax havens) or who are working in other foreign countries and who perform charitable, natural-resource-related, or export-related services to exclude the first $50,000 of foreign-earned income from federal income taxes. This exclusion would replace the current system of deductions to adjust for higher costs of living abroad. The Senate Finance Committee bill would also provide for changes in corporate tax rates and brackets to take effect over a two-year period, as shown in table 3.

Individual taxpayers may deduct 60 percent of any net capital gains from their gross income under present law, so that only 40 percent is subject to taxation. Thus, the highest tax rate for a capital gain of an individual taxpayer is 28 percent (70 percent rate for the top bracket times the 40 percent inclusion of the capital gain in gross income). A corporation pays taxes on capital gains at either a 28 percent rate

4

TABLE 3

CORPORATE TAX RATES AND BRACKETS—
CURRENT LAW AND THE SENATE FINANCE COMMITTEE PROPOSAL

Taxable Income (in thousands of dollars)	Current Law Tax Rates (percentage of taxable income)	Proposed 1981 Tax Rates (percentage of taxable income)	Proposed 1982 Tax Rates (percentage of taxable income)
0–25	17	15	15
25–50	20	20	20
50–75	30	30	25
75–100	40	30	30
100–150	46	40	35
150–200	46	45	40
Over 200	46	45	44

SOURCE: Joint Committee on Taxation, Summary of Tax Cut Proposals, 1980.

or, if it is lower, the rate at which its regular income is taxed. The Senate Finance Committee bill would increase the exclusion for individuals from 60 to 70 percent, thus reducing the maximum possible rate on capital gains to 20.1 percent (67 percent times the 30 percent inclusion). The alternative capital gains tax rate for corporations would fall to 20 percent.

The Senate Finance Committee would, except for public utility property, scrap the present depreciation system in favor of a new plan that would reduce from 130 to 4 the number of asset classes and would reduce asset lives by at least 40 percent, according to some estimates.[5] The plan would assign lives of two, four, seven, or ten years to most assets. "Open-ended" depreciation accounts would replace the current vintage accounts for assets. The value of all assets of a particular life that were acquired would be aggregated in a single permanent account, and the percentage of the balance in the account claimed as depreciation would be subtracted from the balance at the end of the tax year.[6] The remaining amount would carry over to the next year when the same procedure—in effect, a declining balance method of depreciation—would be employed, though new assets would be added to the account as acquired. The amount realized from the sale of used assets would also be subtracted from the appropriate account. The plan would retain an investment tax credit of 10 percent for assets with lives of seven or ten years. A 6 percent credit would be allowed for assets with lives of four years, and a 2.5 percent credit for assets with lives of two years. No tax credit would be allowed for any assets expensed in the year of acquisition up to the $25,000 ceiling for expensing. Structures would be depreciated over twenty years using the straight-line method except for low-income rental housing, which could be depreciated over fifteen years. Owner-occupied business structures could be depreciated over fifteen years using the 150 percent declining-balance method at the option of the owner, subject to application of recapture rules currently applicable to depreciable personal property.

Other features of the bill provide incentives for various activities that affect the economy. The bill would add a 25 percent nonrefundable income tax credit to businesses for their expenditures on research and development that exceed their current R & D expenditures; that is, credit would be allowed for so-called incremental expenditures. The bill would allow a more generous tax credit to businesses maintaining an employee stock ownership plan (ESOP). This provision would allow businesses to calculate the tax credit on the basis of a percentage of payroll instead of on the amount of their contributions to the ESOP at their option. Currently an employee not covered by a tax-qualified pension plan, tax-sheltered annuity, or government pension plan may deduct the amount contributed to an individual retirement account (IRA) up to $1,500 ($1,750 for spousal IRA) or 15 percent of annual wages, whichever is less. This dollar limit would be increased to $1,750 ($2,000 for spousal plans). The bill would also allow those covered by a tax-qualified plan or a tax-sheltered annuity to deduct the amount they contribute to such a plan or to an IRA up to the lesser of $1,000 or 15 percent of annual wages, thus expanding the number who can benefit from these retirement plan deductions.

The present 10 percent tax credit for the rehabilitation of industrial and commercial structures would be increased to 25 percent. The ceiling on the value of used property subject to a 10 percent investment tax credit would be increased from $100,000 to $150,000. The minimum accumulated earnings credit for corporations (before application of a special tax to prevent the improper accumulation of corporate earnings to avoid individual income taxes) would be increased from $150,000 to $250,000, but this increase would not apply to certain service corporations.

THE ADMINISTRATION'S PROPOSAL

President Jimmy Carter announced the administration's economic renewal program on August 28, 1980, a program that would combine additional federal spending on certain initiatives with changes in the tax laws. Draft legislation to effect changes in the tax laws has not been submitted to the Congress, but in broad outline these proposals are as follows.

First, the administration proposes relief from scheduled increases in social security taxes. The social security system is funded by a tax on wages levied on both the employer and employee. Currently the tax rate is 6.13 percent for wage income up to $25,900. The rate will increase to 6.65 percent and the tax base to $29,700 on January 1, 1981, as mandated by the 1977 Social Security Act amendments. The administration proposes that both employers and employees be allowed a nonrefundable credit on their income tax liabilities of 8 percent of their payroll tax payments. This credit would offset the increase in the tax rate but not the taxes incurred because of the higher tax base, and it would be effective for two years during which funding of the social security system would be studied.[7] The administration has proposed that the earned income tax credit (EITC) be raised from 10 to 12 percent and that the phase-out range of $6,000 to $10,000 be raised to $7,000 to $11,000. The administration proposes that when a husband and wife file a joint return, they be permitted to take a deduction equal to 10 percent of up to $30,000 of the lower-earning spouse's earnings. This deduction is the same as that recommended by the Senate Finance Committee after the phase-in period for the latter. The administration would permit Americans living in certain areas abroad to exclude their income from federal taxation, a change designed to promote exports to those areas.

6

The administration proposes a new constant rate depreciation (CRD) plan in lieu of the current system. The CRD proposal would establish three asset classes— one for autos, trucks, computers, and office equipment; a second for machinery and equipment; and a third for buildings. The second class of assets ("Type 2 assets") would be subdivided into twenty-seven categories. All machinery used in glass manufacturing, for example, would be assigned the same depreciation rates, while machinery used for mining and drilling would be given different rates. Type 1 assets have no subdivisions, and Type 3 assets have only two. Thus, many businesses would have only three asset classes, as their equipment would be used for only one type of industry.

Instead of establishing lives for depreciable assets and using various methods of depreciation, as in the current system, the CRD proposal would assign a specific depreciation rate for each asset class applicable to the depreciation base. The CRD proposal would establish open-ended accounts, as in the depreciation plan endorsed by the Senate Finance Committee, and CRD depreciation percentages would be applied to the balances in these accounts. Thus a business would have fewer depreciation accounts than under current law.

This proposal would benefit all assets by a roughly comparable amount, since their treatment would not differ greatly in a relative sense from the treatment they are given under current law. The plan would go into effect immediately so that there would be no transition process. The administration claims that it would increase the allowable depreciation rate by approximately 40 percent. However, the benefit of constant rate depreciation and the applicable investment tax credit could not exceed the benefit of expensing productive assets, that is, writing such assets off in the year of purchase.

The 10 percent investment tax credit (ITC) for an industry's purchase of new plant and productive equipment is available to offset the first $25,000 of taxes due plus 90 percent of the remainder (80 percent in 1981). A major innovation proposed by the administration is that 30 percent of earned ITCs that are not used because a company does not owe taxes be refundable. A special targeted refundable ITC is proposed to cover 10 percent of the cost of eligible investment projects in localities of high unemployment. This credit would be limited to $1 billion a year, and the Commerce Department would issue "certificates of necessity" for projects for which the ITC is authorized. The administration's white paper on its economic renewal program does not specify the criteria to be employed in judging which applications should be granted and which should be denied. The amount of the tax credit would be deducted from the basis for the property, and only the remaining value of the property (90 percent) would be depreciable. Businessmen object to reducing the basis of productive assets by the amount of the ITC and fear that this approach may signal a similar change in the application of the current ITC. Advocates of deduction of the ITC from the basis of productive assets see this approach as reducing the tax cost of the ITC and depreciation. The administration states that it intends to propose tax law changes that will allow small businesses to write off start-up costs.

3

ISSUES AND ARGUMENTS

NEED FOR TAX CUT AND BUSINESS INCENTIVES

Burden of Personal Income Taxes. A prime reason for broad agreement on the need for a tax cut is the increasing burden of federal taxes. Congress has explicitly adopted some federal tax increases, and, in addition, by reducing or eliminating certain deductions and other tax benefits, it has implicitly raised the level of taxes for some taxpayers. A major source of increased tax liability, however, stems from the inflation that has wracked the economy, as distinguished from explicit tax law changes. Salary and wage increases granted to offset part of the effect of inflation provide a greater total income on which individual taxpayers must pay taxes. In addition, inflation-induced wage and salary increases have pushed individual taxpayers into higher tax brackets so that some of their increased income is taxed at a higher "marginal" tax rate. In 1965 one-fifth of individual taxpayers had marginal tax rates of 20 percent, but by 1975 more than half of all taxpayers had marginal tax rates of 20 percent or more.[8] Charls Walker, former deputy secretary of the treasury, notes that "In the 1930s we enacted a personal income tax that was intended to soak the rich, but the progressivity got out of hand because so many people have moved into the $30,000 to $50,000 brackets."[9] Inflation has had far-reaching effects on the amount and distribution of the personal income tax burden. An income increase of 10 percent increases the federal government's tax revenues from the personal income tax by about 16 percent.[10]

Inflation and federal taxes have reduced after-tax real income, according to the Tax Foundation, to its lowest point in any year in the last decade. The Foundation's June estimate concluded that even if taxpayers were to receive a 14.5 percent pay hike in 1980, increased taxes and the reduced purchasing power of their pay would produce a net loss of purchasing power of 1.7 percent.[11] Senator William V. Roth, Jr. (R-Del.) cites Commerce Department data showing that personal income rose 12 percent last year, almost enough to keep up with inflation, but the tax bite increased by 15.8 percent, leaving taxpayers with a gain in income of 8.7 percent, well below the rate of inflation.[12] Congress periodically votes tax cuts to offset partly the average increase in personal taxes due to inflation. Recent tax cuts have not matched the size of inflation-caused tax increases for the average taxpayer. More importantly, according to proponents, these tax cuts fall quite short of offsetting inflation-induced increases in the taxes of taxpayers who fall in higher marginal tax brackets, the ones most likely to invest their income net of taxes in new productive capacity. Unlegislated inflation-caused individual tax increases for fiscal 1981 are expected to approximate $14 billion.[13] Thus there is substantial sentiment favoring a cut in personal income taxes to offset some or all of this increase.

8

Effect of Inflation on Business Taxes. The high rate of inflation during the last several years has affected business to such an extent that the Securities and Exchange Commission has required large corporations to provide information in their annual 10-K reports on replacement cost depreciation and on inventory "profits" due to inflation so that investors and potential investors will not be misled by more traditional financial statements. Our tax laws base the allowable depreciation deduction on the original cost of machinery and other assets employed in the production of goods and services over the anticipated useful life of the assets rather than on replacement costs, but high inflation has made depreciation reserves inadequate to replace these assets. Thus inflation causes an understatement of the costs of operating a business and an overstatement of taxable profits. Adequate depreciation allowances are important to businesses because as much as two-thirds of their capital financing may be derived from such allowances. A study employing 1972 tax data shows that overpayment of business taxes due to inflation varies greatly from industry to industry. The average overstatement at a steady 10 percent rate of inflation was projected to be 25 percent, but railroads, for example, showed an overstatement of 233 percent. Jerome I. Baron of Merrill, Lynch, Pierce, Fenner, and Smith tabulated 1979 data on the effect of inflation on the operating income of 271 companies and found that such income, when adjusted for inflation, declined by 52 percent. It has been pointed out that high inflation rates discourage the adoption of capital-intensive technologies—particularly those that employ assets with relatively long expected lives—and skew investment toward the purchase of inventory and toward capital goods that have short lives.[14] Capital gains taxes apply to inflation-induced (nominal) gains in the value of assets. A capital gains tax must be paid on these nominal gains although the real before-tax rate of return is zero or even negative.[15]

Martin Feldstein and Lawrence Summers of the National Bureau of Economic Research have estimated that in 1977 distortions induced by inflation working through depreciation, false inventory profits, and false capital gains increased taxes on corporate capital by $32.3 billion.[16] Commerce Department data show that actual depreciation for tax purposes fell short of economic depreciation—that is, depreciation at replacement rates—by $14.7 billion in 1977.[17] Although 1971 legislation permits the shortening of asset lives for depreciation purposes by up to 20 percent and permits some acceleration in the amount of depreciation taken in the early years of an asset's life, the complexities involved probably account for the fact that less than one-half of 1 percent of business firms with assets of less than $1 million employed the permissible "asset depreciation range" (ADR).[18]

The inadequacy of depreciation allowances for tax purposes is demonstrated graphically in figure 1. Tax law changes liberalizing depreciation allowances account for the rise in the ratio of depreciation allowances for tax purposes to straight-line depreciation at replacement cost taken in the first twenty years of the post–World War II period. The ratio has declined since the middle 1960s except for a brief period in 1972 when the ADR system became available as an option. Figure 1 shows the decline in the adequacy of depreciation allowances through 1976, when the inflation rate stood at 4.8 percent. The higher rates of inflation since that time would produce an additional and sharper drop in the ratio line in figure 1 if it were extended to 1980. In addition, some economists insist that figure 1 does not fully reflect the inadequacy of depreciation allowances, for it compares such allowances

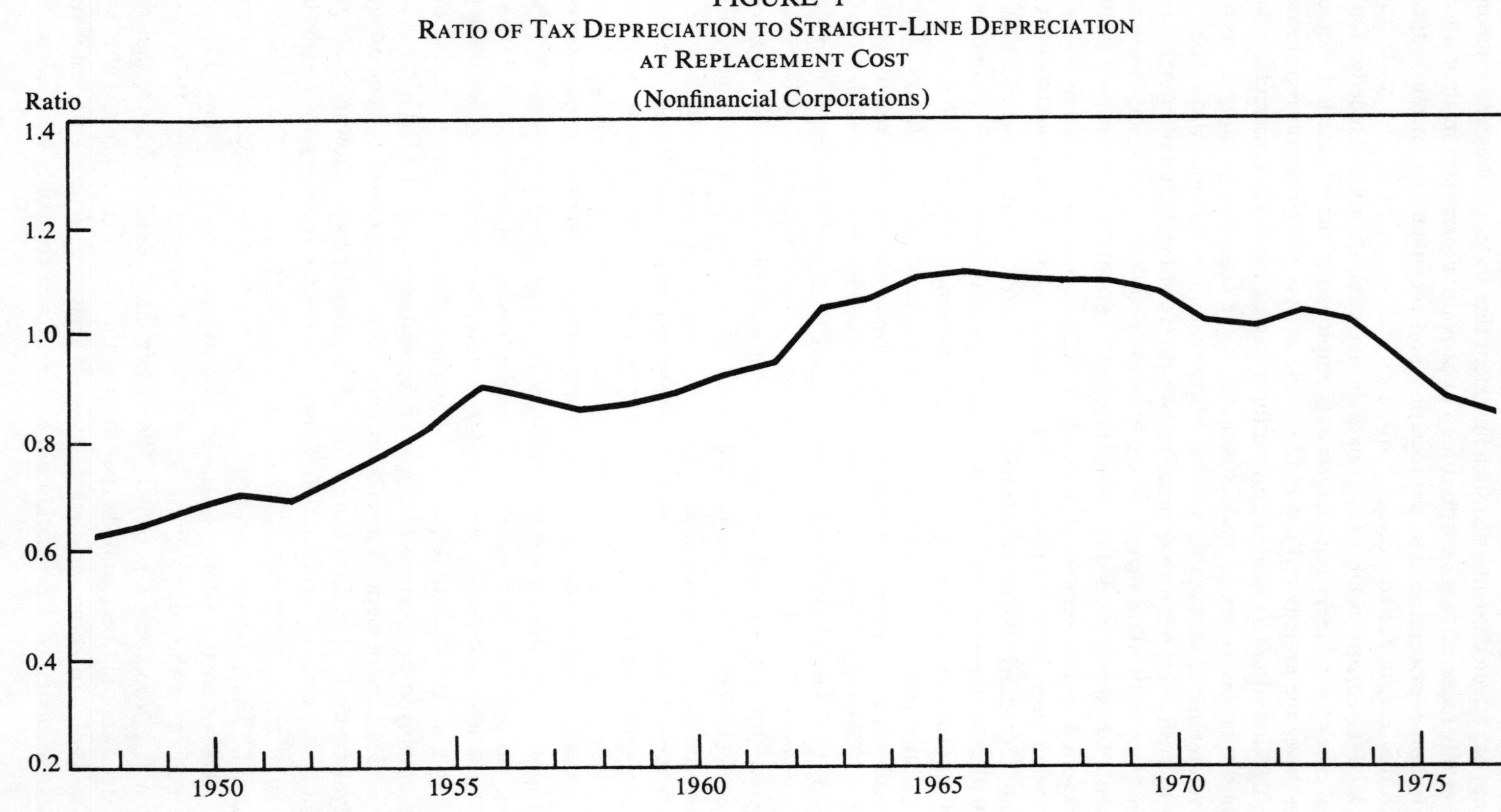

FIGURE 1
RATIO OF TAX DEPRECIATION TO STRAIGHT-LINE DEPRECIATION
AT REPLACEMENT COST
(Nonfinancial Corporations)

SOURCE: Chart 5 appended to statement of Lyle E. Gramley, member, Council of Economic Advisers, before the Subcommittee on Taxation and Debt Management of the Senate Committee on Finance, June 15, 1977. Reprinted from *The Capital Cost Recovery Act Proposal,* Legislative Analysis No. 17 (Washington, D.C.: American Enterprise Institute, 1980), p. 11.

with straight-line depreciation when in fact most productive assets depreciate more rapidly in early years. Thus, the inadequacy of depreciation allowances is claimed to be greater than that shown in figure 1. The inadequacy of depreciation allowances and inflation-induced excess taxation of businesses have stimulated substantial support for tax relief for businesses.

Inflation also results in the taxing of gains from the increased value of inventories, even though this increase may be due solely to inflation. Last-in-first-out (LIFO) accounting mitigates this problem somewhat but does not solve it completely. LIFO accounting, moreover, is costly to install and costly to maintain and thus benefits large firms primarily.

The High Overall Tax Burden and Growth of the Underground Economy. The administration's fiscal 1981 budget projections show that federal tax receipts will continue to climb upward in 1981 not only in absolute terms but also when judged as a percentage of the gross national product (GNP). The steady increase of federal taxes as a percentage of GNP is illustrated in table 4. Revised estimates from a midseason review of the budget, however, show the diversion of even more resources to the federal government. Paul McCracken, a former chairman of the Council of Economic Advisers, notes that federal revenues will rise by $84 billion during fiscal 1981 and that revenues of state and local governments will probably rise by almost $30 billion, for a total increased tax take of about $115 billion as against the administration's estimate of an increase in total national income (which he considers more relevant than GNP) of about $210 billion. In short, according to McCracken, increased taxes will absorb about fifty-five cents of each additional dollar that is earned.[19] Tax increases have far exceeded prices, as inflated as prices are, and tax increases have dwarfed increases in production. A Tax Foundation study shows that an index for all taxes rose 236 percent from 1967 to 1979, while prices rose by 109 percent, and output by only 44 percent. In the heyday of the "tax revolt," taxes rose by 28 percent from 1977 to 1979, prices by 16.8 percent, and output by 7.6 percent.[20]

A growing number of people, disturbed by the growth in taxation and government regulations, deal in cash as much as possible and fail to report income or report only part of their incomes. Estimates of the magnitude of this underground economy and federal tax losses as a consequence of it vary substantially. Internal Revenue

TABLE 4

FEDERAL BUDGET RECEIPTS
AS A PERCENTAGE OF GNP (1976–1981)

Year	Percent of GNP
1976	18.5
1977	19.4
1978	19.5
1979	20.1
1980 (est.)	20.8
1981 (est.)	21.7

SOURCE: Executive Office of the President, *The Budget of the U.S. Government—FY 1981*, p. 612.

Service noncompliance estimates for 1976 placed unreported income for that year at $75–100 billion and the tax loss at $13–17 billion. The General Accounting Office has criticized this estimate of unreported income as too low by perhaps $50 billion. Peter Gutmann, professor of economics and finance at Baruch College, criticizes the omission from the Internal Revenue Service (IRS) estimate of barter, skimming of expense accounts, thefts from business, and numerous illegal activities. Others believe that the unreported income of aliens in this country may be substantially understated. Representative Al Ullman (D-Oreg.), chairman of the House Ways and Means Committee during the 96th Congress, puts tax losses due to tax evasion at $35 billion a year. Whatever the appropriate figures for unreported income and the resulting tax losses—and some estimates are much higher than those cited here—many students of the situation are convinced that a growing number of persons are concealing income and are failing to pay an increasing amount in taxes in reaction to high marginal tax rates.[21] Other persons react to high marginal tax rates by increased use of tax shelters to reduce or avoid tax liability. Although people in higher income tax brackets may be able to make investments that yield lower before-tax returns, legal, accounting, and syndication fees are often enormous and investment risks may be high. The costs of avoiding taxes may often be only marginally lower than the cost of paying taxes. A reduction of marginal tax rates, according to some scholars, may induce high-income taxpayers to engage in more taxable activities, thus leaving both the taxpayers and the U.S. Treasury better off while increasing the efficiency with which our productive resources are used.[22] Lower marginal tax rates are also seen by some as one means of encouraging those participating in the underground economy to come above ground and report taxable income.[23]

Economic Conditions and Problems with Productivity. The downturn of the economy beginning in April and May 1980 has been a cause of concern to many economists and policy makers. Some industries were more hard hit than others. Production in the automobile industry fell by 18.6 percent from March to May 1980; primary metals production declined by 15.5 percent over the same period; and the total productive capacity that manufacturing industries utilized fell from 82.8 percent to 77.6 percent.[24] Overall, real GNP declined by 9.6 percent in the second quarter, and the unemployment rate rose from 6.2 percent in March to 7.8 percent in May.[25]

Paul McCracken, noting the diversion of 55 percent of increased (marginal) earnings to various governments because of higher taxes, contends that taxes are so high at the margin "as virtually to assure a leaden, arthritic, creaking economy."[26] Other observers claim that the economy is receiving inadequate stimulus. In measuring discretionary fiscal policy, a common tool used in Keynesian theory is the "high-employment budget." Because changes in the federal surplus or deficit are due in part to cyclical changes in the economy, a budget deficit per se does not indicate fiscal stimulus or restraint to economists who favor use of the high-employment budget, which estimates the levels of receipts and expenditures that would obtain if the economy were on its *potential* growth path. (At this time, that budget would imply a 5.1 percent rate of unemployment.) In 1975, for instance, the actual deficit was $70.6 billion, but the high-employment deficit was $18.2 billion, the difference being caused by the high unemployment rate and the negative growth experience.[27]

Economists who rely on the high-employment budget claim that it removes the effects of boom and recession and thus it is a better measure of the stimulative or restrictive effect of fiscal policy. The administration's 1981 budget estimated that the high-employment budget would yield a surplus of $57 billion in that fiscal year.[28] Data Resources, Inc., estimated a $51 billion surplus, and Walter Heller, former chairman of the Council of Economic Advisers, estimated the 1981 high-employment surplus to be about $75 billion in the absence of a tax cut. Heller concludes from these figures that "the fiscal drag is huge." [29] Thus, although there will be a deficit in the actual budget, indicators such as the full-employment budget, the unemployment rate, and the retarded growth of GNP are cited to justify a tax cut for fiscal 1981. Heller, citing the greatly increased tax take, argued in late June that we are in the midst of one of history's sharpest swings toward fiscal restriction and thus he did not wonder that fiscal moderates and conservatives support what he referred to as a modest $30 billion federal tax cut.[30]

A persistent problem in the U.S. economy that affects this country's ability to bring inflation under control and to compete successfully with other industrialized nations in international trade is our declining rate of growth in worker productivity. The United States has the lowest rate of growth in productivity (the rate by which output per worker increases) of any major industrialized nation except the United Kingdom. The rate of growth in the United States from 1973 to 1979 was half the rate of growth for the period 1960 to 1966 and is still declining. A number of causes may account for this decline, but one that stands out is our low rate of saving and low rate of investment in more efficient machinery and technology that would enable our workers to produce more per hour of labor. Americans are saving less of their disposable income than citizens of other industrialized countries, partly as a result of inflation and partly because of our tax system that encourages consumption and discourages capital formation. Total investment as a percentage of GNP is less in the United States than in other industrialized nations, but, more seriously, as Martin Feldstein, president of the National Bureau of Economic Research, points out, a large part of our smaller investment share is invested to replace existing facilities, to buy housing, and to accumulate inventories, so that only 3 percent of GNP is devoted to expanding productive capacity.[31]

In sum, inflation and our tax system reduce the level of private saving and investment and thus retard the nation's rate of economic growth. The interaction of inflation with our consumption-oriented tax system also creates distortions that impose serious efficiency losses on the U.S. economy. They divert resources from superior to inferior economic uses in response to the large differentials imposed on different sectors of the economy and on different industries. They divert work effort from productive activities to the search for ways to minimize the erratic and hard-to-predict effects of inflation on tax burdens. And, they discourage work effort undertaken to save for future consumption.[32] Thus, many policy makers place a high priority on adjustments in our tax system to spur growth in productivity. This analysis will examine how each of the three major tax proposals before the Congress seeks to achieve this objective.

Critics of the pending tax cut proposals do not disagree in general that there is a need for tax relief, but they do disagree as to the appropriate timing of tax relief and the extent and nature of the relief to be given. These critics argue that the proposed cuts are costly and will make it more difficult to balance the budget. They foresee a serious threat of additional inflation from the tax cuts, and they dispute the effectiveness of the plans in promoting saving and investment in productive capacity and their effectiveness in promoting increased productivity as claimed by proponents. These arguments are discussed in the following section.

OVERALL EFFECT OF TAX REDUCTIONS

Particular features of the three major tax cut proposals will be compared in a subsequent section. This section will examine the general arguments as to the effect of substantial tax cuts. One measure that would redirect a greater portion of our resources toward productive capital investment, in the effort to increase productivity and achieve related goals, would be to reduce government spending, deficits, and borrowing. Charles Schultze, chairman of the Council of Economic Advisers, acknowledges the need to turn resources back from the government to the private sector, and proponents of the Republican tax cut proposal have specifically endorsed this goal.[33] None of the three major tax cut proposals, however, makes adoption contingent on cuts in government spending, and advocates of the proposals presumably favor adoption of their plans with equal or somewhat lessened enthusiasm even if spending cuts are not accomplished. Accordingly, this analysis will not examine specific proposals for reduction in spending or assume spending reduction of a set percentage.

Cost of Tax Reductions and Effect on the Budget. A key concern of some policy makers is the cost of the various tax cut proposals in terms of forgone revenues. The estimated costs of the three proposals are outlined for fiscal years 1981 through 1985 in tables 5–7. Cost projections for the Republican proposal are shown in table 5. Some advocates of this proposal contend the tax losses from depreciation reform are overstated because the Treasury has overestimated the number of firms that will be able to offset greater depreciation benefits against tax liabilities; that is, firms without profits would not benefit.

TABLE 5
STATIC REVENUE LOSS FROM THE
REPUBLICAN TAX REDUCTION PROPOSAL
(billions of dollars)

Feature of Bill	1981	1982	1983	1984	1985
Tax rate reductions of approximately 10 percent for individual taxpayers	18.9	34.2	40.6	47.4	54.6
10-5-3 depreciation	2.0	7.6	17.4	32.3	49.7
Total	20.9	41.7	58.0	79.7	104.3

NOTE: Years are fiscal years. Data assume the bill takes effect on January 1, 1981. Details may not add to totals because of rounding.
SOURCE: Office of the Secretary of the Treasury, Office of Tax Analysis.

TABLE 6

STATIC REVENUE LOSS FROM THE SENATE FINANCE COMMITTEE TAX REDUCTION PROPOSAL

(billions of dollars)

Feature of Bill	1981	1982	1983	1984	1985
Increased personal exemption	1.7	4.9	5.1	5.4	5.6
Increased zero bracket amount	1.0	1.6	1.6	1.7	1.8
Increased earned income credit	0.1	0.6	0.5	0.5	0.5
Marriage penalty deduction	0.3	3.4	6.8	8.3	9.7
Personal rate reduction	7.9	14.3	17.2	20.9	25.0
Depreciation and ITC reform	4.3	13.7	18.6	19.0	19.7
Corporate rate reduction	1.0	3.5	5.5	6.3	7.1
Capital gains tax cut	0.8	2.7	3.0	3.2	3.6
Small-business tax cuts	0.1	0.3	0.2	0.2	0.2
R & D, savings and export incentives	1.0	2.6	3.9	3.8	2.8
Total	18.2	47.3	62.5	69.4	75.9

NOTE: Years are fiscal years. Details may not add to total because of rounding.

SOURCE: Joint Committee on Taxation, Summary of Tax Cut Proposal (H.R. 5829) and revisions of September 19, 1980.

TABLE 7

STATIC REVENUE LOSS FROM THE ADMINISTRATION'S TAX REDUCTION PROPOSAL

(billions of dollars)

Feature of Proposal	1981	1982	1983	1984	1985
Social security tax credit	3.8	19.3	15.7	17.5	20.1
Earned income credit changes	[a]	0.9	0.8	0.8	0.7
Marriage penalty deduction	0.3	5.2	6.0	7.1	8.0
Investment tax credit changes	0.2	3.1	3.5	3.3	3.3
Constant rate depreciation	2.8	9.0	14.3	18.4	22.2
Other changes	0.2	0.4	0.4	0.5	0.6
Total	7.3	37.9	40.7	47.6	54.9

NOTE: Years are fiscal years.

[a] Less than $50 million.

SOURCE: Office of the Secretary of the Treasury, Office of Tax Analysis.

The Senate Finance Committee proposal would be somewhat more expensive than the Republican proposal in the second and third years following enactment, but it would be less expensive in out years, as shown in table 6. Static revenue losses from adoption of the 10-5-3 depreciation reform proposal contained in the Republican plan may be higher or lower than the losses shown in table 5, depending on the scholar providing the estimates.[34]

The Senate Finance Committee proposal involves a smaller personal income tax reduction than the Republican plan. Business tax reductions, when all features of the bill are considered, would exceed those of the Republican plan during the first three years following enactment. Senator Russell B. Long (D-La.), chairman of the Senate Finance Committee, when he acknowledged his preference for the depreciation reform plan of Senator Lloyd M. Bentsen (D.-Tex.), added that Congress could switch to the more generous 10-5-3 plan in three years.[35]

The administration's proposed changes in business tax laws, including tax credits to offset social security payroll taxes, would be almost as expensive as those in the Senate Finance Committee bill. The administration's economic renewal plan, however, includes spending proposals as well as tax cuts. If additional spending for second and subsequent years matches that proposed for the first year of the administration's plan, the total cost of business benefits under the administration's plan would exceed those provided for business in the Senate Finance Committee plan.[36] Relief for individual taxpayers would be less than under either of the other proposals. Table 7 outlines the cost of the tax cut features of the administration's plan.

Critics of substantial tax reductions contend that if we accept the view that cutting taxes will reduce government revenues, then a tax cut must be "paid for" either by reducing expenditures (or slowing their rate of increase) or by an increase in the deficit. The hard choices that must be made in the present period of severe budgetary tightness are demonstrated by the projections of Rudolph G. Penner, director of tax policy studies for the American Enterprise Institute. Penner states that "The proceeds of automatic tax increases and energy taxes, including the new gasoline tax, could be returned to the public and the receipts-GNP ratio could be restored to its level in 1979 [20.1 percent] if we were willing to tolerate a deficit in 1985 of 0.6 percent of the GNP, or $26 billion. Conversely, spending could be lowered by almost this amount if we had no health or welfare initiatives before 1985."[37] Of course, these kinds of estimates may change depending on the performance of the economy. According to a midsession review in 1980, the 1980 budget is estimated to be in deficit by $60 billion and the 1981 budget is projected to be in deficit by nearly $30 billion.[38] Some oppose tax cuts primarily because they fear the consequences of substantial budget deficits. Penner states:

> Spending is truly out of control in both the legal sense that outlays can and will soar without new legislation and in the more technical sense that they cannot be forecast with any accuracy from one quarter to the next. . . . Until some concrete signs appear that the spending process is under control or that tax revenues have caught up with the uncontrolled path, I reluctantly conclude that there should not be any tax cuts in our near future.[39]

Others oppose tax cuts because they may not leave room in the budget for certain spending priorities. Representative Paul Simon (D-Ill.) warns that "the loss of revenue from the tax cut would eliminate any cushion that would allow us to provide needed funds for veterans' benefits and other worthwhile federal programs and still balance the budget."[40]

Senator William Proxmire (D-Wis.) contends that tax cuts should be "earned" and that Congress should reduce federal spending to offset the cost of the tax cuts. Some sponsors of substantial tax cuts do advocate spending cuts that would make room in the budget for tax cuts.[41] Other advocates of tax cuts contend that Congress has had ample opportunity to cut spending to make room for tax cuts but that it has not been equal to the task. Thus, it is necessary to cut taxes to make it more difficult for Congress to spend freely. Such a reduction, it is claimed, would help limit federal spending because of the political embarrassment of deficits. Representative John J. Rhodes (R-Ariz.) argues that cutting taxes will help control spending by exposing the bloat and waste in the budget and that with as much as one dollar out of ten wasted, per a statement of the attorney general, there obviously is room in the budget to provide for a tax cut. Senator Dole claims that the tax cuts proposed really are not tax cuts but are merely "tax abatement," since they will only moderate the additions to the tax burden caused by inflation and scheduled increases and will not provide a real reduction in the tax burden.[42]

Advocates of supply-side theory contend that the static loss in revenues projected by Treasury estimates fails to take into consideration the feedback effect of tax cuts. Supply-side advocates contend that as marginal tax rates are reduced and greater production raises supply in the marketplace, the tax cut is self-financing at least in part. A 1979 study of the Kennedy tax cuts is said to show only a small revenue loss from the individual income tax by 1966, a loss largely offset by gains in corporate, state, and local tax receipts owing to added economic growth. Although the magnitude of the feedback effect is often hard to determine, a general rule of thumb applied by some economists is that in time slightly less than 40 percent of the initial tax loss will be recovered through added taxes made possible through growth of the economy.[43] The Treasury Department, on the other hand, estimated the feedback effect of the 10-5-3 depreciation reform proposal, for example, at 30 percent of the revenue loss from that plan.[44]

Advocates of a cut in the capital gains tax rate, such as that found in the Senate Finance Committee proposal, note that while the Treasury opposed the 1978 capital gains tax cut and claimed that it would reduce revenues by $2.2 billion in 1979, the Treasury subsequently acknowledged that the tax cuts increased capital gains realizations by about $8 billion, which reduced its estimate of revenue loss for 1979 to $1.3 billion. Representative Steven D. Symms (R-Idaho) contended that Treasury Department evidence indicates that 75 percent of the static revenue loss projected has actually been recovered through increased investor gains.[45]

Effect on Inflation. Most of those opposing a tax cut do not disagree that the tax level is high, and many concede that a tax reduction will eventually be needed to reduce this burden. Standard Keynesian macroeconomic analysis would show, according to opponents, that a tax cut, particularly a cut in individual taxes, will stimulate aggregate demand, since personal disposable income will rise and most of that increase will be spent on consumption items. Although there may well be some increases in the labor supply and investment, supply-side measures are unlikely to be effective quickly enough, according to critics, to prevent an increase in inflation. The administration contends that GNP cannot grow fast enough over the next five years to balance the budget and hold down inflation at the same time. In other words, the productivity gains of a tax cut are likely to be long term and uncertain while the inflationary consequences are likely to be immediate and substantial.[46] Paul A. Volcker, chairman of the Federal Reserve Board, contends that financial markets have become so sensitive to inflation and so wary of budget deficits that just the anticipation of higher spending relative to tax receipts would drive interest rates higher. Thus, in his view, tax reduction would have to be conditioned on cuts in federal spending if risks of additional inflation are to be avoided, and a $633 billion second budget resolution, such as that voted by the Senate in August, would not be the kind of spending plan that could accommodate a noninflationary tax cut.[47]

Critics of a substantial tax cut at this time contend that when sales prospects brighten, as they typically do after a tax cut, there is greater demand for investment funds to increase productive capacity, but at the same time the government would borrow additional money to finance a part of the greater deficit in the budget because of the tax cut. This competition for funds would force an increase in interest rates and would exacerbate the inflation that is our most serious domestic problem. The tax cut proposals present a choice, according to critics, between higher interest rates and lower taxes.

> Most people would welcome lower taxes, but for a great many Americans a drop in interest rates is far more urgent. That's true for farmers and small businessmen. It's true for people who want to buy houses and for the people who want to build them. High interest rates are severely aggravating the manifold troubles of the automobile industry. While a tax cut will be necessary next year for economic growth and higher employment, a tax cut this year is less important than getting interest rates down.[48]

Alfred Kahn, chairman of the Council on Wage and Price Stability, argues that the Republican proposal, which would provide more tax relief to individual taxpayers than to the business sector, would put more money into one side of workers' pockets while taking those dollars out of the other side through inflation.[49]

Senator George J. Mitchell (D-Maine) cites the particular burdens that rising inflation induced by a tax cut may cause.

> Inflation strikes all Americans, regardless of their tax burdens. It affects those on social security, who have no tax burden. And it affects the unemployed, whose incomes are too low to incur a tax liability. A tax cut will not and cannot give any relief to these people. But the inflation that this tax cut will unleash will undoubtedly have an effect on these people.[50]

Personal income tax cuts are the ones that are most inflationary, according to critics of tax cut proposals.[51] The administration's tax cut proposal, which would provide a smaller percentage of tax relief to individuals, is defended by Chairman Schultze of the Council of Economic Advisers as a stimulus program that would add about 1 percent to the growth of real GNP in 1981 and another 1 percent in 1982. This, Schultze argues, would return the growth rate of real GNP to 4 to 5 percent a year, which he claims would be sufficient to promote recovery but would not be so large as to set off inflationary pressures.[52]

Richard Lesher, president of the Chamber of Commerce of the United States, and Richard Rahn, chief economist of that organization, contend, however, that the administration's individual tax cut proposal would be more inflationary than either of the other two tax cut plans, for it would benefit primarily persons with lower incomes who are more likely to spend rather than save their tax savings than is true of other taxpayers. Senator Orrin G. Hatch (R-Utah) contends that targeted tax benefits such as earned income tax credits, larger personal exemptions, and the zero-rate bracket amount features of the tax cut plans of the administration and the Senate Finance Committee have little or no effect on the marginal rate of federal taxes and thus would not provide supply-side incentives, would not stimulate productivity, and thus would not combat inflation.[53]

Advocates of tax cuts reject the claim that the risk of added inflation should delay action on tax cut legislation. Senator Dole states that the attempt to balance the budget through massive tax increases has failed and that high tax rates have crippled economic growth and have thrown millions of people out of work. He contends that unemployment will not balance the budget, but that it will only produce more federal spending, less federal revenues, and huge budget deficits, as every 1 percent increase in the unemployment rate produces a $20 billion increase in the budget deficit. He advocates cutting taxes to break the vicious circle of higher taxes, more unemployment, more spending, and more budget deficits.[54] The General Accounting Office notes that some commentators believe that our slow rate of capital formation is responsible for the increase in the inflation rate, the deficit in our balance of trade with other countries, and rising unemployment. The key to curbing inflation, according to Michael Evans, president of Chase Econometrics, is to increase productivity by encouraging businesses to step up capital investment through lower tax rates.[55]

Supply-side advocates contend that reducing the marginal rate of taxation for individuals will bring more labor into the marketplace, thus stimulating additional production; that additional capital investment stimulated by business tax cuts will make laborers more productive, thus adding to production and the supply of goods in the marketplace; and that this increased supply will lower unit prices, increase exports, and strengthen the dollar, thus neutralizing inflation. Any tax cut that causes more goods and services to be produced will be anti-inflationary, according to these tax cut proponents, if the money supply is tightly controlled. A reduction in marginal tax rates increases savings, it is claimed, and thus lowers pressure on interest rates. Tax cuts will broaden the tax base, and the feedback effect of such cuts will dampen the risk of inflation from budget deficits.[56] Additional arguments of supply-side advocates are discussed in the next subsection.

Senator Bentsen argues that the depreciation reform plan now incorporated in the tax cut proposal of the Senate Finance Committee is an effective way to hold down inflation. Senator Long argues that the Senate Finance Committee bill will not trigger a new inflationary spurt but will encourage jobs and, in response to the Treasury secretary's criticism of across-the-board tax cuts as inflationary, Senator Long cites the tax cuts proposed by President Kennedy—which he claims expanded production and balanced the budget—as being appropriate for the current situation.[57] Using a supply-side model, Otto Eckstein of Data Resources, Inc., estimates that raising the business investment tax credit from 10 percent to 12.7 percent and accelerating the tax depreciation of business equipment by four years would reduce the consumer price index by 4 percent by the end of the decade. He believes that the administration's tax cut proposal would encourage investment and therefore would reduce the nation's basic inflation rate by 0.6–0.7 percent in four years. White House domestic policy adviser Stuart E. Eizenstat contends that reducing the social security tax burden on business as proposed by the administration would cut labor costs and would lower inflation. He estimates that this change alone would lower consumer prices by 0.2 percent by the end of 1981.[58]

Advocates of a major tax cut claim there is still another reason why their proposals should not be inflationary. Citing the $114 billion in new tax burden that will be effective in fiscal 1981 (see the subsection "The High Overall Tax Burden and the Growth of the Underground Economy"), advocates claim that the tax cuts they propose would only partially offset these increases, so that traditional predictions of inflation cannot be credited. An even larger tax cut in the range of $50–70 billion would not be inflationary, according to Leon Taub, senior analyst for Chase Econometrics, particularly since the economy is in a hole.[59]

Many proponents of a tax cut insist that, while some people judge the adequacy of a tax cut by how well it offsets the effects of inflation, the real goal should be a tax system that encourages the most efficient allocation of society's resources. See the section on "Impact on Business Resource Allocation."

Critics of a major tax cut now contend that proponents' reliance on experience with the Kennedy tax cuts is misplaced. See the fourth paragraph of the section "Targeted Individual Tax Cuts versus Across-the-Board Cuts."

Effect of Plans on Incentives to Save and Invest. President Carter, in announcing his economic renewal program, stated that the most important step we can take to revitalize American industry is to provide incentives for greater private investment.[60] Specific industries that need to expand to meet national goals and international trade objectives or to modernize their obsolete equipment and facilities will have unusually heavy capital demands. The administration's goal of a major shift in the use of energy to coal resources that calls for doubling annual coal production by 1990 and tripling production by 2000, for example, will require at least $26 billion in constant dollars between now and 1990, according to the president of the National Coal Association, and more than twice that amount by the year 2000 to meet capital investment requirements. These amounts compare with total coal industry capitalization of about $12 billion at the present time. The capital-intensive coal mining industry requires approximately $330,000 of investment for each additional coal mining employee. Neil Goldschmidt, secretary of transportation, estimates that suppliers to U.S. automakers will need $80 billion in capital to retool over the next five years.[61] Other industries will require large additional investments.

Each of the three major tax cut proposals seeks to encourage investment by a combination of business and personal tax cuts and tax benefits. The particular changes proposed will have a bearing on the proposals' effectiveness. A comparison of the particular features of the three proposals as they relate to incentives for saving and investment will be discussed in a subsequent section. All three proposals, for example, seek to modify the handling of depreciation for tax purposes, a reform that provides significant targeting for investment in productive capacity. Paul McCracken makes the case for general tax cuts by stating:

> The first step for fiscal policy if we are to encourage economic progress, instead of economic arthritis, and ultimately reach balance in the budget is direct action on taxes so that a dollar is worth earning and saving and investing. Without such action the probability of urgently needed economic revitalization is low, and without that economic revitalization the probability that the budget will be balanced is close to zero.[62]

Restoration of incentives for earning and saving is the central argument of policy makers and economists who favor tax cuts. The Congressional Budget Office agrees that general cuts in tax rates for individuals can substantially increase aggregate saving, although the extent to which these savings are invested in new plant and equipment for productive growth depends on the after-tax rewards offered by various investment opportunities.[63] Targeting significant tax benefits to businesses that produce industrial output will, it is claimed, make such businesses more profitable and the after-tax returns of such businesses will enable them to attract needed investment funds. The administration's tax cut proposal would provide a higher proportion of tax cut benefits to the business side than the other two plans—55 percent of the first year cuts and more than the usual one-third allowed to businesses in past tax cut legislation.[64]

A significant and growing number of policy makers and students of economic policy advocate what is popularly known as "supply-side economics." This school of thought contends that we have attacked our economic problems by stimulating demand for too long. Increasing demand without increasing the efficiency and capacity of our productive industries to meet demand, it is claimed, has contributed to inflation, and the current unsatisfactory economic situation. Past policies have promoted demand and consumption at the expense of work and saving, it is said, because a dollar earned is taxed when earned and taxed only lightly by sales and excise taxes when it is spent on consumption items (an average of 4.9 percent per one study). A dollar earned that is devoted to saving, on the other hand, is taxed when earned. The income from the dollar invested is taxed heavily as it yields corporate profits, dividends, interest, or capital gains (an average of 56.1 percent according to one study), and, if the invested dollar is eventually spent, it is subject to sales and excise taxes. Thus, in that case, there is no net tax penalty for immediate consumption as compared with investment and eventual consumption.[65]

What is needed, according to supply-side advocates, is to promote policies that increase the supply of goods in the market by encouraging saving and investment in productive capacity. Such policies will, in the absence of improper expansion of the money supply, lower price levels as more goods are produced to meet demand. A properly designed tax cut, according to supply-side proponents, involves cutting *marginal* tax rates (not necessarily average tax rates), for the marginal tax rate determines the share or percentage of any additional income earned that the taxpayer may keep. Cutting marginal rates, according to this view, will cause people to substitute work for leisure and saving for spending on consumption items. When taxes go up, the steep progression of marginal tax rates, it is claimed, greases the rungs of the ladder of opportunity and thus discourages those who would otherwise work harder and produce more to climb that ladder. Leisure then becomes cheaper in terms of forgone income. Supply-side advocates contend that cutting marginal tax rates has the opposite effect—it makes leisure and current consumption more expensive in terms of the income that people must give up to engage in these activities, it makes the rewards of saving and investment greater, and thus it encourages saving and investment.[66]

While many observers do not subscribe to all of the tenets of supply-side economics, there is much support for the view that appropriate tax cuts can stimulate saving and investment. The chairman of the Council of Economic Advisers claims that the administration's proposals will boost real investment by 10 percent by the end of 1982 and by as much as 14–15 percent by 1985. The president of the

Chamber of Commerce of the United States claims that if the 10-5-3 depreciation plan and related investment tax credits are adopted, the American steel industry can be competitive with that of Japan by 1985. More advantageous depreciation provisions in the tax law provide more internally generated funds for investment by the businesses employing those provisions. A Data Resources, Inc., study commissioned by the Committee for Effective Capital Recovery found that in the fifth year of the 10-5-3 depreciation reform proposal—the first year in which it would be fully phased in—real business fixed investment would be $20.9 billion higher than under current policy, and that over the phase-in period it would be $10 billion a year higher on average, which represents an increase of 5 percent.[67] To justify tax cuts in the current economic climate, some economists and advocates of supply-side theory point to the results of the corporate and personal tax rate cuts and investment tax credit pushed by President Kennedy. Economists Dale Jorgenson and Robert Hall examined the tax incentives for investment adopted during the 1950s and 1960s and concluded that the effect of the acceleration of depreciation was substantial, especially for investment in structures; the effect of shortened asset lives was significant for equipment; and the effect of the investment tax credit of 1962 was dramatic.[68] Lyle E. Gramley, when a member of the Council of Economic Advisers, contended that business investment plays a dual role in our economic system by directly creating jobs and income in the capital goods industries and in the businesses that supply them. As capital investment adds to demand it also increases supply. Gramley contends that because business investment affects both demand and supply, it plays a crucial role in the achievement of the nation's economic goals.[69] While proponents of tax cuts to stimulate saving and business investment may differ as to the magnitude of the investment that will be caused by specific tax proposals and may not agree on all aspects of the theory as to how tax cuts stimulate business investment, they insist that stimulus for investment is needed, as the United States spends only 9 percent of its national income on capital investment, while West Germany spends 15 percent and Japan 20 percent.[70] Changes in the tax laws can provide investment stimulus, according to proponents.

Critics of major tax cuts to spur saving and investment contend that investment is close to historical highs already, even after adjustment for pollution control equipment. (Proponents, on the other hand, claim that it is net investment that determines the growth of the capital stock and net investment is below its historical highs.) Critics maintain that in any event capital investment is not a tax issue and that cutting taxes will not guarantee that tax savings will be invested in productive equipment and facilities. Offering tax benefits may simply reward investments that would have been made in any event. Investment in new productive equipment and facilities is more influenced, according to some critics of major tax cuts, by the expectation of growing markets, and if businesses do not anticipate substantial market demand for their products, the availability of investment funds is not likely to cause them to expand productive capacity.[71]

Some critics argue that a "supply-side" tax cut will produce no miracle cure because individuals with higher after-tax incomes due to a tax cut may prefer to take time off and work less rather than more and thus will have no more money to save and invest. In any event, it is argued, private saving in this country has remained remarkably stable at about one-fifth of total savings, and although incentives may coax private savings up by perhaps 2 percent, there is not much prospect for more saving than this. Even if individuals do save more, it is claimed that there is no automatic link between their saving and business use of the savings for improved efficiency in and increased capacity for industrial production. Additional individual savings may be routed into additional housing or into consumer goods, assets that may have less effect on productivity goals than investment in business plant and equipment. Some scholars contend that reducing the cost of capital may indeed induce additional investment, but its effects may be gradual and of uncertain magnitude. Saving in periods of recession, it is argued, may only serve to increase unemployment and may actually reduce capital formation.[72]

The Hall and Jorgenson study on the effect of tax law changes in the 1950s and 1960s assumed that certain variables such as interest rates remain constant. Critics contend that such variables may not remain constant, and if the federal government finances any part of the tax cut revenue loss from Treasury borrowing, this action will put upward pressure on interest rates, and higher rates will inhibit investment. Some economists claim that if the cost of tax cuts and investment tax credits is financed by selling government bonds rather than by cutting expenditures, total industrial investment may decline as Treasury borrowing may soak up investment funds and, at a minimum, the method of financing the cost of tax cuts will be important in determining the effectiveness of the tax cut strategy. Even if firms increase their investment in manufacturing equipment and facilities as a result of tax cuts, it is argued that increased production will drive prices down, and lower prices will discourage production and new investment somewhat.

Representative Augustus F. Hawkins (D-Calif.) contends that use of the term "supply-side economics" to justify a tax cut is a smoke screen that reveals nothing. In his view, supply is called forth by demand and effective demand needs to catch up with our present supply capabilities before investment in new plant and equipment is encouraged by government tax cuts. The tax cut stimulus should be reserved to encourage the manufacture of products that are in short supply, according to Representative Hawkins, and should be limited to the production of commodities whose manufacture is in the national interest.[73]

Advocates of a substantial tax cut respond to the claim of critics that personal savings do not fluctuate greatly regardless of incentives by citing recent studies showing a significant savings response to higher rates of return. One economist, for example, estimates that a 10 percent increase in the real rate of return on savings will generate approximately a 4 percent increase in savings. The reliance of some critics on demand-side theory is rejected by proponents of a tax cut as adherence to a failed policy. Advocates cite the conclusion of the General Accounting Office (GAO) that, except in conditions of deep depression, demand stimulus alone does not raise the rate of capital formation.[74] Without net capital formation, advocates maintain, we cannot compete against foreign imports, cannot effectively compete for sales in foreign markets, or provide a better life for our own citizens.

Critics maintain that the view that individuals add substantially to personal savings in response to higher rates of return on savings is a minority view.

Effect on Productivity. One of the principal goals of the tax cut proposals, particularly the provisions to set more favorable depreciation terms for business assets, is to increase capital investments over the long run and thus to increase the productivity of labor. All things being equal, improved productivity will increase output in the economy, lower the price level, and improve our standard of living. Improved productivity would have important implications not only for the domestic economy but also for international trade by U.S. firms and for the U.S. trade balance. Senator Lloyd M. Bentsen (D-Tex.), a sponsor of the depreciation reform legislation that was included in the tax cut legislation reported by the Senate Finance Committee, argues that:

> One of the primary reasons for lagging productivity is a lack of capital for modernizing the productive capacity of this country. We need to put new tools in the hands of American workers. But we will not get those new tools until people are willing to invest in them. Faster depreciation is a very efficient method to encourage the investment needed to boost productivity.[75]

The General Accounting Office notes that capital formation is essential to economic growth, that jobs and improved productivity depend on it. Those who suffer most from the lack of economic growth, it is claimed, are those who are already at the bottom of the economic ladder. The rate of increase in capital available per worker, according to the GAO, declined by approximately two-thirds in the 1970s, and this sharp decline contributed to the sluggish rise in labor productivity in this country and retarded the normal rise in the American standard of living. The 1979 Economic Report of the President notes that capital accounted for 0.69 percent of the growth in the economy from 1953 to 1964, when the ratio of real investment to real GNP averaged 9.07 percent. Edward F. Denison states that capital's contribution rose to 0.94 percent for the period from 1964 to 1969 when the investment-to-GNP ratio increased to 10.27 percent. A similar increase of 0.25 percent in capital growth today would equal $6 billion in GNP. Representative Toby Roth (R-Wis.) contends that the United States has lagged behind other major industrial nations in capital investment. Japan invested twice as much of its GNP as we in the United States did during 1960–1978, and during the 1970s Japan's rate of productivity increased by an average of 2 percent a year. In the modern economy, according to the GAO, technical progress and capital formation are the two means by which we add to productive capacity. Capital formation facilitates technological progress by embodying technical advances in new capital goods.[76] Lyle E. Gramley, a member of the Federal Reserve Board, notes that tax incentives to stimulate business investment appear to be the surest way to increase aggregate capacity to produce. He predicts that the administration's tax proposals would increase productivity 0.4 percent per year. Otto Eckstein of Data Resources, Inc., employed a supply-side model to estimate that raising the business investment tax credit from 10 to 12.7 percent and accelerating the tax depreciation of business equipment by four years would increase productivity by 3.3 percent.[77]

Yale professor James Tobin, a former member of the Council of Economic Advisers, contends on the other hand that only limited improvements in productivity can be attained by increasing investment and that the returns in added consumption from such a program are long delayed. Brookings economist George Perry claims the nation's bad productivity performance of recent years cannot be changed drastically through the tax system. The Congressional Budget Office acknowledges that tax policies to encourage savings are not likely to have a large impact on productivity within the first five years of enactment.[78]

Economist Robert Eisner argues that many factors affect productivity and that to see higher investment as a panacea for the productivity problem is a mistake. Economist Barry Bosworth notes that "factors which do not necessarily increase with higher capital formation accounted for 80 percent of U.S. growth between 1948 and 1969 with increased capital inputs contributing 20 percent." [79] Denison contends that higher employment was a major factor influencing the growth rate in the late 1960s and that this influence increased productivity by four times the rate of capital additions.[80]

Proponents of tax cuts to promote investment and increase productivity respond that increased investment is required to support increased employment. Even though productivity can be stimulated by means other than increased capital investment, these proponents argue, our rate of growth in productivity is so low and our manufacturers are at such a disadvantage in coping with imports and competing for a larger share of the world market that we cannot ignore any method of improving productivity. Our ability to utilize other factors to improve productivity is limited, it is argued, but, increased capital investment will in fact increase the growth rate of productivity.

Critics contend that tax incentives may be an expensive way of improving the rate of productivity growth for reasons stated in the subsection "Cost of Tax Reduction and Effect on the Budget."

ADVANTAGES AND DISADVANTAGES OF
SPECIFIC FEATURES OF PROPOSALS

Comparison of Depreciation Plans. Depreciation allowances under current law, which are based on historical value and on expected asset lives, fall far short of providing adequate sums for the replacement of capital items. Depreciation reform strikes at only one of the factors that cause businesses to be taxed more heavily in times of inflation than otherwise. The three major tax cut proposals recognize the inequity of current depreciation law and attempt to simplify its compliance requirements. This subsection will compare how well the three proposals would simplify depreciation, relieve the effects of inflation, and affect resource allocation by businesses. See the section "Overall Effect of Tax Reductions" as to the stimulation of additional capital investment.

Simplifying depreciation. The class life asset depreciation range (ADR) was introduced in the early 1970s to provide depreciation reform, but it proved to be so complex in application that a sampling of 1974 tax returns showed that under 1 percent of businesses with assets of less than $1 million used ADR. Treasury estimates indicate that less than 0.4 percent of all businesses with less than $500,000 in depreciable assets use ADR.[81] Even larger businesses spend a greater sum on the services of lawyers and accountants than would be necessary but for the complexities of the tax law dealing with depreciation. The three tax

25

cut bills differ in their approach to depreciation reform, as can be seen from the chapter "Tax Cut Proposals."

All three proposals would abandon the some 130 classes of depreciable property currently employed. The Republican proposal would narrow equipment classifications to two. Equipment would be depreciable in either five years or three years. Special rules would apply to utility property.

The Senate Finance Committee bill would narrow the classification of most depreciable property to four classes. Assets with six and a half years of ADR guideline life or less would be recoverable in two years; those with ADR lives of seven to eleven and a half years would be recoverable in four years; assets with ADR lives of twelve to sixteen and a half years would be recoverable in seven years; and assets with longer ADR lives would be recoverable in ten years. Businesses could elect annually the rates of depreciation to be employed in that declining balance system. An optional alternative would be provided for depreciable real property, however, and utilities would continue to use present law, except that the ADR variance for utility property would be increased from 20 to 30 percent.

The administration's bill would feature constant rate rather than variable rate depreciation. The administration's plan provides two classes of assets for equipment and a third for buildings, but Type 2 equipment assets would be subdivided into twenty-seven categories, each for a particular industry, and Type 3 building assets would be divided into two categories. A firm that engaged in one line of business might find itself concerned with only two categories of assets because of the industry orientation of Type 2 classifications.

The 10-5-3 plan is applauded for its simplification in substituting shorter arbitrary lives for assets rather than adhering to the useful-life concept, a concept referred to as obsolete by the chief economist for the Chamber of Commerce of the United States. The Senate Finance Committee plan and the administration's plan are more closely related to the useful-life concept than the 10-5-3 plan. Representative Kemp considers the Senate Finance Committee plan to be a sixth as complicated as the administration's proposal and claims that 10-5-3 is a tenth as complicated as the administration's plan. Advocates of the two criticized plans contend, however, that substantial accounting simplification is accomplished in these plans through open-ended rolling accounts that avoid separate recapture rules, whereas the 10-5-3 plan requires a separate annual account for each class of assets. The National Federation of Independent Business argues, however, that small businesses lack the accounting manpower to use the complex 2-4-7-10 method incorporated in the Senate Finance Committee bill. Critics of 10-5-3 contend that the phase-in of that plan adds complications not present in the other plans. Representative Barber B. Conable, Jr. (R-N.Y.) contends that the administration's proposed pooling of 130 asset classes into 30 depreciation classes still leaves its depreciation plan too complicated and that its expansion of the ADR system is pointless because small businesses do not use ADR now.[82]

Advocates of the Senate Finance Committee plan cite the allowance of the complete write-off or expensing of the first $25,000 of investment in equipment and machinery in a year as an additional simplification for small business that will enable some businesses to avoid accounting for depreciable property. Representative Clarence J. Brown (R-Ohio) points out, however, that small businesses will not take advantage of this proposed simplification because the Senate Finance Committee bill denies the benefit of the investment tax credit to properties expensed under this provision and the firms would be better off financially to depreciate their property over the required period of time and to take advantage of the credit. Critics of the administration's constant rate depreciation plan contend that since the benefit of depreciation and the investment tax credit cannot exceed the benefit of expensing, additional complications would be involved in calculating the alternative benefits.[83]

Effectiveness in providing relief against the effects of inflation on business taxes. Various plans have been advanced for neutralizing the effect of inflation on business taxes. Comprehensive indexing of the tax system for inflation could completely offset inflation-induced tax increases for businesses and could provide the stability and certainty that would encourage investment in productive equipment and facilities. Martin Feldstein, president of the Bureau of Economic Research, contends that replacing the historic cost depreciation method with an indexed depreciation system would raise the after-tax yield on all prospective projects and, at the current high rate of inflation, this approach would offer a greater stimulus to investment than the 10-5-3 depreciation reform plan.[84] A Library of Congress analysis is cited by others to show that it would be simpler and more efficient to repeal the investment tax credit and allow immediate expensing or charge-off of assets, after a phase-in period.[85] The complications of indexing are cited to show that small businesses might not take advantage of indexing if it were optional.

The depreciation changes advanced in the three major tax cut bills do not go so far as to scuttle depreciation and investment tax credits in favor of indexing or the immediate expensing of capital assets. Thus the question is: To what extent do these plans adjust for inflation-induced tax increases? When Feldstein compared the 10-5-3 depreciation reform plan and indexing of the current ADR system, he found that in most relevant ranges of inflation, interest rates, and asset lives, the value of 10-5-3 was within 10 percent of the value of indexing.[86] Robert McIntyre of the Tax Reform Research Group estimated the effects of 10-5-3 depreciation reform as well as those that would be achieved by expensing and concluded that the tax benefits of 10-5-3 and the investment tax credit were 103 percent of those that would be provided by expensing.[87] The 10-5-3 depreciation reform, however, would not do as well as indexing or expensing in adjusting for inflation-induced tax effects if we were to experience an even higher rate of inflation. Thus, 10-5-3 lacks the flexibility of either indexing or expensing.

Both the Senate Finance Committee plan and the administration's proposal purport to shorten asset lives by about 40 percent for depreciation purposes; neither would offset the effect of inflation on all types of capital assets. These plans, which include other proposed business tax changes, would cost approximately two-thirds as much as 10-5-3 in forgone business tax revenues in the fifth year. (See tables 5–7.) Thus, their supporters claim that these plans could be accommodated within the budget more easily without cutting popular spending programs. John Kendrick, a former chief economist of the Commerce Department, contends, however, that the administration's program would only increase the ratio of fixed business investment from 10 to 11 percent of GNP when what is needed is an increase to 12 percent. William Freund, senior vice-president and chief economist of the New York

Stock Exchange, also believes that the administration's program would not provide a sufficient rate of growth for the nation's business economy and asserts that to claim that the proposal can generate incentives for capital investments much beyond the level of normal recovery is both optimistic and unrealistic. In similar vein, Cliff Massa, vice president for taxation and fiscal policy of the National Association of Manufacturers, singles out the four-year class life under the Senate Finance Committee plan for criticism, contending that since business could claim only a 6 percent investment tax credit for assets of this class, the plan would provide no "juice" to stimulate investments of this category.[88] The administration's plan, on the other hand, would allow the 10 percent tax credit for assets with lives longer than one year. Thus, for very short-lived assets it may provide substantial offset to inflation-induced tax increases and an incentive to invest in such assets rather than in others. See "Overall Effects on Tax Reductions" for additional arguments as to the general effect of tax cuts on inflation and productivity. Many advocates of a tax cut insist that even if depreciation changes offset the effect of inflation on depreciation allowances perfectly, there would still be disagreement as to the tax plan that would best promote economic efficiency. See the section on "Impact of Business Resource Allocation."

Impact on business resource allocation. Differences in taxes on various assets and industries reduce economic efficiency and lower output below that which would be possible if the influence of taxes were neutral. The current depreciation system is not a neutral one. It contains a fairly strong bias in favor of shorter-lived equipment assets, largely because of the investment tax credit. Jane Gravelle of the Congressional Research Service has calculated that the effective tax rate for equipment is lowest for those assets with lives of six to ten years—their effective tax rate is about half of the tax rate for equipment having twenty- to thirty-five-year lives. Inflation introduces additional biases into our system. Nicholas Tideman and Donald Tucker calculated that for nonfinancial firms of $1 million and more in assets a continued 10 percent rate of inflation causes average tax overpayments of 25 percent. For certain industries, however, these overpayments are much higher: 48 percent in communications and utilities, 92 percent for airlines, and 233 percent for railroads.[89]

Many economists favor a system that eliminates distortions of this kind to improve economic efficiency. According to Gravelle, the 10-5-3 system would reorient the tax system toward favoring long-lived equipment assets and it may more than offset the present bias in favor of short-lived assets.[90] Feldstein agrees that the present bias in favor of short-lived equipment would be countered by 10-5-3 as 10-5-3's "bias toward longer-lived investments is slightly stronger than the bias toward shorter-lived investments that prevails under existing rules." [91] Firms that are capital-intensive and that have longer-lived assets, such as primary metals, communications, public utilities, railroads, shipping, and oil pipelines, would stand to benefit most. Those receiving the smallest relative benefit from 10-5-3, according to the Treasury Department, would be construction, motor vehicle manufacturers, services, agriculture, wholesale and retail trade, fabricated metals, and electronics.[92] The administration's plan, on the other hand, may stimulate investment in very short-lived assets because the 10 percent investment tax credit, as already noted, would apply to assets with lives in excess of one year.

The Senate Finance Committee depreciation plan and the administration's plan would introduce some additional biases into the distribution of tax benefits from depreciation because fewer classes of assets would be employed and such a reduction necessarily reflects a change to a more arbitrary schedule of asset lives. Because the lives selected represent an adjustment derived from existing ADR lives, however, such a schedule would make fewer changes in existing biases than the 10-5-3 plan would. Critics of the administration's plan insist that it will result in disparate treatment among industries, since the same item of equipment may be used in different industries but each of twenty-seven different industries will have its own depreciation rate. This disparity, according to critics, may cause inefficiencies owing to less generous treatment for a particular item of equipment in some industries and overgenerous treatment in others.

The 10-5-3 depreciation reform proposal has been criticized because of the reduction of the life of structures to ten years. Individual taxpayers in higher income tax brackets obtain greater benefits from depreciation of structures than those in lower brackets do. The 10-5-3 plan would permit 44 percent of the cost of a structure to be written off through depreciation the first year, compared with 21 percent under current law. This provision would permit larger tax losses in early years, which investors could then offset against income from other sources, and in later years they could unload the investment property as depreciation allowances declined. Critics question the need for more accelerated depreciation for structures, since structures may appreciate in value rather than depreciate, as in the case of equipment. Some critics claim that the 10-5-3 proposal would stimulate the sale of depreciation allowances. Representative Charles A. Vanik (D-Ohio) opposes 10-5-3 because, among other reasons, he believes we need new machine tools and industrial processes, not new buildings.[93]

Advocates of the 10-5-3 depreciation plan contend that the inclusion of structures is necessary to offset the bias that would otherwise obtain against retail and service establishments that have less to gain from the plan than manufacturing and other capital-intensive industries. Retailers and service establishments have most of their fixed investment in real estate.[94] The National Association of Manufacturers defends the inclusion of commercial structures in the 10-5-3 plan on the ground that industrial structures are an integral part of the productive process. Former Treasury Secretary Michael Blumenthal contends that investment in structures in January 1978 was 11 percent below the peak reached four years ago.[95] Thus, it is claimed, a liberal tax benefit may be necessary to reverse this trend and to aid the retail and service industries.

The Senate Finance Committee bill would allow the taxpayer to continue with existing depreciation arrangements or to elect straight-line depreciation over a shorter period of time, but it would not permit separate depreciation of building components if the election is made. Only owner-occupied structures would be entitled to depreciation over a fifteen-year period on the basis of a 150 percent declining balance. The alternative depreciation plan, according to the Senate Finance Committee, would provide greater simplicity (composite depreciation would be required in lieu of separate depreciation of components) and more rapid depreciation than is currently available.[96] Since the declining balance method of depreciation under the election would be limited to owner-occupied buildings, proponents believe that the practice of buying and selling depreciation entitlements will not be unduly encouraged. Critics of the treatment of owner-occupied structures in the Senate Finance Committee's bill object to its discrimination against leased property and to the application of total depreciation recapture (the so-called section 1245 recapture rule) to general-purpose real estate.[97] In general, the administration's plan would shorten asset lives by about 40 percent over ADR lives.

The 10-5-3 depreciation reform plan would be particularly helpful to public utilities, since it favors industries with long-lived assets. Governor Hugh Carey of New York cites the huge capital needs of utilities for coal conversion, pollution abatement, and replacement of obsolete equipment as justifying the benefits of 10-5-3. Critics contend that 10-5-3 is too generous and represents a major departure from past depreciation practice that would shorten asset lives for utilities more than for most industries. The Senate Finance Committee's bill would reduce the life of depreciable public utility property, but only by increasing to 30 percent the 20 percent variance permitted from ADR lives.[98] The administration's proposal would generally shorten asset lives by 40 percent of ADR lives.

Many advocates of a tax cut insist that the rhetoric about providing incentives for saving and investment is misplaced. They claim they are not seeking special incentives, but rather a neutral tax system that would remove the disincentives to saving and investment that have been identified earlier in this section. Removal of these disincentives, according to these advocates, would end the loss to society that now occurs because of the misallocation of resources. Individuals and businesses would then be free to make consumption and investment decisions in a neutral tax environment, and this would produce a far more efficient allocation of resources. Many business critics of the current depreciation system argue that the best depreciation plan would be one that approximates the results that would be achieved by the expensing of productive assets.

Refundable Income Tax Credits for Businesses. The administration, as a part of its economic renewal program, has proposed that the regular investment tax credit be made refundable to the extent of 30 percent and that a targeted and fully refundable investment tax credit be established for those who invest in declining areas and who qualify for Commerce Department certificates of necessity. These proposals will be discussed in order.

Currently some businesses cannot gain the benefit of investment tax credits because they do not have any federal tax liability against which the credits can be offset. Present tax law recognizes that this situation may obtain in some years and thus allows credits to be carried back three years and forward seven years on the assumption that sufficient taxes will be payable during that eleven-year period to permit most business firms to gain the advantage of the tax credit for expenditures in new productive facilities and equipment. The administration champions the refundability of 30 percent of the regular investment tax credit to boost investment in new equipment, claiming that the refundability of the credit would reduce the uncertainty of a business concerning its ability to use the credit. Rapidly growing firms, firms experiencing cyclical downturns, and newly organized firms with start-up losses typically cannot use all of their investment tax credits. The administration claims that the major beneficiaries of the refundable credit would be primary metal manufacturers, electric utilities, railroads, and auto manufacturers. It expects this program to cost $2.5 billion in forgone revenues in fiscal 1985.[99]

Advocates of refundability claim that the present nonrefundable credit tends to place new and marginal businesses at a competitive disadvantage. New firms typically do not incur tax liabilities for several years, since start-up costs frequently exceed their incomes and such businesses have cash-flow problems in their early years. It is no help, advocates claim, to tell these firms that they can benefit from a nonrefundable credit by offset against taxes owed seven years after they need the credit to help pay the cost of machinery and equipment. Some firms, it is argued, suffer losses not because of poor management but because of economic conditions over which they have no control. The nonrefundable credit is inequitable, it is asserted, because two firms may make identical investments but one firm can claim the credit, whereas the other cannot. Advocates claim there is precedent for refundability as in the case of tax credits for solar and wind energy property. They note that the credit is directly linked or targeted to investment and that the refundable credit avoids the administrative burdens and headaches that come with management of a loan guaranty arrangement in the style of the Chrysler Corporation rescue.[100]

Opponents of refundability for 30 percent of the investment tax credit point out that the program would merely become another government spending program. Such a program adds to the budget deficit and, according to critics, is not an appropriate part of the tax program. Opponents maintain that the proposal represents a "creeping bailout mentality" and that it would lock capital into industries that are not performing well. Such capital could be put to more productive use elsewhere. There is no mechanism in the tax credit proposal to differentiate between the bailout of inefficient or bad management and assistance to others. The plan, according to opponents, would bias investment incentives toward investment in low-income companies, so that some companies might manipuate their activities and tax records to gain the largest government handouts possible at the same time they pay large salaries and bonuses to inefficient management.

Other critics of the refundable tax credit proposal contend that the proposal would create a bad precedent. The greatest efficiencies in our economy are said to be achieved when firms compete in the marketplace rather than compete with their tax lawyers. The free market, they argue, provides for the most efficient appropriate allocation of economic resources. Government spending programs and their sequel, the refundable tax credit, do not. The refundable tax credit program, it is claimed, would reduce productivity, not improve it. A free market economy requires that businesses with bad management be allowed to die just as businesses with good management should be allowed to prosper. A refundable tax credit would expand the welfare concept to businesses, it is claimed, and institutionalize bailouts in place of the present case-by-case consideration by Congress. We should not, in this view, provide for an automatic bailout of ailing firms such as Chrysler Corporation.[101]

The second program of refundable tax credits proposed by the administration calls for bonus tax credits of an additional 10 percent targeted to distressed areas. The Commerce Department would issue qualifying certificates of necessity to certain eligible projects within a $1 billion annual ceiling, and the certificates would expire within five years if the plant and equipment involved were not placed in use within that time. The tax credit would be fully refundable (rather than 30 percent refundable as in the administration's first proposal), and it would be a supplement to other programs targeted to distressed areas, for example, the economic development administration program and urban development action grants. These programs, proponents claim, would bring vitality to declining areas that are hit with the loss of industry. President Carter's announcement of the economic renewal program asserted the need to provide strong incentives for businesses to invest and create jobs in areas threatened by economic decline. Governor Carey advocated even larger (25 percent) partly refundable tax credits to promote investment in distressed areas with state designation of the areas that would be targeted in certificates of necessity issued by an economic revitalization board.[102] The Senate Finance Committee bill would increase the existing tax credit from 10 percent to 25 percent for the rehabilitation of industrial and commercial structures in an effort to help revitalize urban centers. That credit, however, would not be refundable.

Opponents of refundable tax credits for investments in certain areas raise many of the same objections to this program that they raise against partial refundability of the regular investment tax credit. In addition, they note that the program may reward some companies needlessly, since they would have made the investments in any event, and all of us will be subsidizing such windfall benefits through the federal tax system. Economist Michael L. Wachter of the University of Pennsylvania maintains that if we pick and choose on a sectoral basis, we will end up with constituency politics. Then productivity will certainly fall. Most dividends of projects financed with refundable tax credits, it is claimed, are likely to be political. Critics noting that the president's announcement referred to aid to "threatened" areas point out that most areas can claim to be threatened in one way or another, even from fair competition. Limiting assistance through this program to concerns that obtain a certificate of necessity from the Commerce Department will simply mean, according to opponents, that projects will be chosen on a political basis, for politicians will see the program as a rich vein of funds to be directed toward favored constituencies. If investment decisions are fragmented and decentralized in the competitive free marketplace in the American tradition, one mistake is not everyone's mistake. The same cannot be said, it is asserted, when a government agency decides which projects to fund and which to deny. The targeted tax credit proposal, according to opponents, shifts investment decisions to Washington that should be left to private enterprise in the free market. If more power over investment flows to Washington, opponents insist, more investment money will flow away from its most productive uses.[103]

Other Business Tax Adjustment Proposals. This subsection will discuss the arguments for and against the principal tax changes offered in the three tax cut proposals to stimulate business investment and improved productivity. The 10 percent investment tax credit is a significant business incentive. Currently the credit may be used to offset all of the first $25,000 of tax liability, 80 percent of the remainder for the taxable year ending in 1981, and 90 percent for taxable years ending in 1982, or thereafter; 100 percent of the credit may be taken for property with a useful life of seven or more years, 66⅔ percent for property with a useful life of five or more but less than seven years, and 33⅓ percent for property with a useful life of three but less than five years.[104] The 10-5-3 depreciation reform proposal would provide a 10 percent credit for Class 1 property depreciable over ten years and for Class 2 property depreciable over five years, and a 6 percent credit for Class 3 property depreciable over three years. (Class 3 assets exceeding $100,000 in value would be carried as Class 2 assets.) The Senate Finance Committee proposal would provide a 10 percent tax credit for assets depreciable over either ten or seven years, a 6 percent credit for those depreciable over four years, and a 2.5 percent credit for those depreciable over two years. These latter percentages would also apply to property not subject to the new cost recovery system, primarily public utility property. The administration proposes that all new qualifying property with a useful life of more than one year be eligible for the full 10 percent investment credit. Neither the Senate Finance Committee proposal nor the administration's proposal would shorten asset lives as such as much as the 10-5-3 proposal, and the administration proposal eschews acceleration of depreciation in early years for constant rate depreciation. Thus, overall, the investment tax credit and depreciation reform employed in the 10-5-3 proposal is the most favorable program to businesses financially and the administration's plan is the least favorable. Of course, the Senate Finance Committee proposal employs other incentives that will encourage investment such as corporate tax rate reduction, capital gains tax cuts, widening the tax brackets, and the R & D tax credit.

The Republican 10-5-3 proposal with investment tax credit taken from the Jones-Conable bill and coupled with individual tax rate cuts was offered as a simplified proposal that might win early acceptance during the 96th Congress, whereas a more complicated plan would be more controversial. Since its backers on the Senate Finance Committee voted to report the alternative tax cut plan submitted by the committee majority and since Governor Reagan endorsed the alternative plan, failure of the Republican plan to provide for some or all of the options and alternatives contained in the other two proposals should not necessarily be taken as opposition by the 10-5-3 sponsors to the Senate Finance Committee options. Most businesses continue to prefer the 10-5-3 plan over the depreciation provisions of the other two plans.

The Senate Finance Committee bill includes two additional provisions for investment tax credits. The present 10 percent rehabilitation tax credit would be increased to 25 percent to help upgrade factories, office buildings, and retail and wholesale stores that have been in use at least twenty years. Sponsors contend that this credit will provide special assistance to older industrial sections of the country. The administration proposes fully refundable tax credits limited to $1 billion in certificates of necessity issued by the Commerce Department. (The advantages and disadvantages of refundability for business tax credits are discussed under "Refundable Income Tax Credits for Businesses.") The Senate Finance Committee bill would also raise the ceiling on the amount used equipment may benefit from the 10 percent investment tax credit from $100,000 to $150,000 to ensure that small business participates in the upgrading of productive facilities that the bill is intended to stimulate. More small businesses than major corporations rely on the purchase of used equipment.[105] The ITC provided under the other two tax cut plans would benefit investment in both new and used productive assets.

The Senate Finance Committee bill provides for a nonrefundable 25 percent income tax credit for research and experimental expenditures that exceed the average of such expenditures during a base period. The credit, expected to cost $0.2 billion in fiscal 1981 and $0.5 billion in fiscal 1982, is proposed because businesses are reluctant to increase expenditures for such activities when subsequent earnings from such activities may not be directly identifiable. Since real research expenditures in the United States have declined as a share of GNP, the committee wishes to increase incentives for greater private research activity. Rather than tax credits, the administration's bill would provide direct expenditures of $0.6 billion for fiscal 1981 and 1982 for research activities.[106]

The combination of accelerated depreciation and the investment tax credit, according to Laurence N. Woodworth, assistant secretary of the Treasury before his death, has a greater short-run effect on investment per dollar of forgone revenue than either corporate tax rate cuts or elimination of the double tax on dividends. This combination of tax benefits is considered to be more effective than other benefits in encouraging investment in modern equipment, which in turn improves the long-run ability of the economy to achieve economic growth without adding to inflation. The tax credit reduces, in practical effect, the purchase price of equipment and increases the net cash flow after taxes to the investor. It is beneficial to small businesses because it aids cash flow immediately.[107]

Those who favor other investment incentives contend that the investment tax credit subsidizes the use of resources for particular purposes and thus tends to remove some decisions affecting the allocation of resources from determination by marketplace forces. The tax credit may in some cases, it is claimed, affect the capital intensity of the production process without augmenting volume of production. The credit may increase the demand for capital, and unless provision is made to increase the supply of capital, the stimulus to investment may raise interest rates. The tax credit, as opposed to corporate tax rate cuts, favors capital-intensive industries but does little for retail and wholesale businesses. Five-year accelerated depreciation under the 10-5-3 plan combined with the 10 percent investment tax credit is claimed by some to be more generous than expensing, which is the equivalent of exempting those assets from income taxes. Many businesses view the 10-5-3 plan and its proposed tax credits as more favorable than the other plans, whereas critics argue that 10-5-3 and its credits are more costly than other plans and leave less room in the budget for spending programs. Some critics argue that the credit may not contribute to long-term growth in some cases because the investments would have been made even without the credit.[108]

The Senate Finance Committee bill would cut both individual and corporate capital gains tax rates so the highest individual rate on capital gains would be 20.1 percent. The alternative capital gains tax rate for corporations would be reduced to 20 percent. Advocates of this change argue that high capital gains rates lock investors into assets when economic efficiency would dictate greater freedom to sell and reinvest in other assets. The committee argues that high rates have contributed to slower economic growth and have reduced the incentives to make investments, particularly risky investments in relatively new firms and industries. Lower rates would promote increased mobility of capital funds and more economic activity, which in turn would limit the loss of revenue from this change as more asset sales would be consummated and thus more taxes would be collected. See the last paragraph of the section "Cost of Tax Reduction and Effect on Budget." Lower rates would also offset some of the tax take owing to inflation gains, as distinguished from real gains in the value of assets. Advocates see this proposed change as a significant aid to small business in obtaining venture capital, whereas critics see this cut as benefiting investors and corporations who are more able to bear the tax burden than wage earners, and as reducing the revenues available to fund social programs.[109]

The Senate Finance Committee bill would cut the top corporate income tax rate by 2 percent and widen the tax brackets in a manner that would aid small businesses. Critics of this approach to business tax relief contend that such a reduction does not guarantee that the money saved will go into investment for additional productive equipment and facilities, for it can be put into cash flow, into the bank, or into higher dividends. Obviously cuts in the corporate tax rate do not benefit unincorporated businesses. On the other side, it is argued that corporate taxes increase the incentive toward debt financing and earnings retention as capital invested in the corporate sector is taxed twice and, according to the General Accounting Office, the resulting disincentives to investment in corporations produce inefficient allocation of the stock of capital, which has been estimated by some to have reduced national output by $4–6 billion in 1976. Thus tax cuts are favored to stimulate capital investment. Arthur Burns, former chairman of the Federal Reserve Board, would prefer a sharp reduction in the corporate income tax to changes in business depreciation because such a reduction would work impartially for both labor-intensive and capital-intensive industries, whereas depreciation changes would not. Thus a cut in tax rates would help small businesses that are generally not capital-intensive while depreciation reform would give them much less tax relief.[110]

Tax Credit for Social Security Payroll Taxes. The administration's economic renewal program anticipates that for a two-year period wage earners and employers would be allowed a tax credit of 8 percent of social security taxes paid. The credit would be refundable to employers, including state and local governments and non-profit organizations. It would not be refundable to wage earners. Employers who take the tax credit would not be allowed the normal deduction for the payroll taxes covered by the credit. The Social Security Act amendments of 1977 call for an increase of the social security tax from 6.13 percent to 6.65 percent on January 1, 1981, for both employees and employers; the amount of earnings subject to the tax will increase from $25,900 to $29,700. The payroll tax will increase to 6.70 percent in 1982; payroll tax increases are expected to add revenues of $16.6 billion in fiscal 1981 and $23.4 billion in 1982.[111] The tax credit would not fully offset the increased taxes generated by the payroll tax. The credit would cost $19.3 billion in forgone revenues in fiscal 1982, for example (per table 7), but the payroll tax would raise revenues of $23.4 billion in that year.

Advocates of a tax credit to offset all or part of the social security payroll tax increase claim that two-thirds of the benefits of the tax credit would flow to individuals. Such relief would in effect substitute revenues from the progressive income tax for the moneys generated by the regressive payroll tax, according to proponents.

35

This equivalent of a payroll tax cut would be more "progressive" (it would provide more benefits to those earning between $5,000 and $10,000 than those earning larger sums) than an across-the-board income tax cut, which would benefit taxpayers in higher brackets more than it would benefit low-income taxpayers.[112] (For a discussion of whether individual taxpayers should receive tax rate cuts proportionate to their tax payments or on some other basis, see the subsection "Targeted Individual Tax Cuts versus Across-the-Board Cuts.")

Stuart Eizenstat, White House domestic policy adviser, argues that a tax credit offsetting business payroll taxes is a means of lowering labor costs to employers and thereby a means of lowering inflation. In his view, adoption of the administration's proposal would put consumer prices at the end of 1981, 0.2 percent below where they would be otherwise. The Congressional Budget Office has made the same projection for the effect of the 10 percent (rather than 8 percent) refundable tax credit proposed by Representative Richard A. Gephardt (D-Mo.) and Senator Bill Bradley (D-N.J.). The projection of the Congressional Budget Office is based on the assumption that 75 percent of the reduction in the employers' share of the payroll tax would be passed on to consumers in lower prices in the first year. One estimate concludes that if the increase in social security payroll taxes legislated in 1977 were completely rolled back—the approach favored by Representative Henry S. Reuss (D-Wis.), for example—by 1982 real GNP would be 1 percent higher and the GNP deflator (a measure of inflation) 0.5 percent lower than at present.[113]

Advocates of the tax credit rely upon its effect on overall employment to win support for it. Adoption of the credit would reduce the cost of employing workers and would benefit labor-intensive businesses in particular. Representative Gephardt estimates that his proposal, which is somewhat more generous than the administration's credit, would increase overall employment by 250,000. Advocates contend that this sort of targeting is preferable to the remedy chosen by the Senate Finance Committee to offset inflation and the payroll tax, namely, cutting the individual income tax rate, increasing the personal exemption, and so forth. Senator Bradley argues that it takes an investment of about $100,000 in the manufacturing sector to provide for each new employee but in the service sector an investment of only $20,000-40,000 is required for this purpose. Thus he views the tax credit as offering a great opportunity to assist employers that are most likely to employ minorities, women, the unskilled, and others who are most seriously hurt by the recession.[114]

The administration's estimate of the cost of the tax credit proposal is shown by fiscal year in the first line of table 7. Alternatives not yet determined would take the place of the credit after two years. Advocates of the credit contend that the cost in forgone revenues—$19.3 billion in fiscal 1982, for example—is misleading inasmuch as there will be offsetting savings from the employment of perhaps 200,000 people. These savings would be realized, according to proponents, because each 1 percent increase in the unemployment rate increases the 1981 budget deficit from $23 billion to $31 billion.[115] In other words, the tax credit may save approximately $5.4 billion because 200,000 more persons may be employed than would otherwise be the case.

Opponents of the administration's proposed tax credit, which would offset most of the increase in payroll taxes adopted to finance social security, deny that indirect substitution of general revenues to pay a part of the cost of this program will make its financing "progressive" in nature. In fact, according to opponents, the payroll tax system was found in an earlier study to be progressive to the middle of the income scale and regressive thereafter. Increasing the wage base, however, is said to make the incidence of the tax still more progressive. Until 1971 only $7,800 of a worker's wages were taxable, but the wage base now stands at $25,900 and is scheduled to rise to $29,700 in 1981. In other words, according to opponents, financing through the payroll tax is increasingly progressive and the administration's proposed tax credit would aid wage earners in these higher brackets. On the other hand, wage earners with the lowest incomes will not benefit from the administration's proposed credit because they pay no income tax against which the tax credit can be taken as an offset. The tax credit is not refundable to these low-income wage earners, although it is refundable to employers.[116]

A more serious objection to the tax credit, according to opponents, is that it would establish a precedent for general revenue funding for a part of the cost of the social security program and would change the essential nature of the program from a contributory retirement system to a welfare program. Once the tie to payroll financing is broken (the tax credit uses tax funds that now go into general revenues to offset payroll taxes), opponents claim, Congress will lose all restraint in voting benefit improvements and an ever-increasing portion of social security financing will be from general revenues. The tie to payroll tax financing is important, opponents of the tax credit maintain, for Congress exercises a measure of restraint in voting payroll tax increases because of public awareness of the bite of the payroll tax and, like any prudent family, it keeps the benefits authorized within the revenues, at least on a pay-as-you-go basis. Chairman Volcker of the Federal Reserve Board, noting his familiarity with the reasons that the administration wishes to provide a tax credit, nonetheless maintains that it would be dangerous to break the link between full self-financing of the social security program through payroll taxes, and argues that if we broke this link, we would regret it. Some critics of the tax credit proposal point to a nationwide survey through personal interviews of attitudes toward social security to show that general revenue financing really is not required, as only about 25 percent of those interviewed thought that social security taxes were too high considering the benefits provided by the program. Critics also point out that compared with workers in other leading industrial nations, American workers indeed have a light payroll tax burden, according to a recent publication of the Department of Health and Human Services. The German workers' share of the tax was 16.4 percent in 1979 compared with 6.13 percent for the American worker, and the German employer had to pay about the same amount. In Japan the worker's share of social security taxes in 1979 was 9.1 percent, in France it was 12.04 percent, and in the Netherlands it was 23.42 percent. Advocates of the tax cut proposed by the Senate Finance Committee insist that that plan provides adequate relief to wage earners without tampering with the self-funding nature of the social security system. Critics of a higher income level than is true now. Critics of the social security tax credit security system if it ceases to be fully contributory and that workers currently feel secure in knowing that their contributions will fund benefits for their old age, a form of enforced saving.[117]

Advocates of the social security tax credit claim that the burden of the social security tax credit on the lowest paid workers has not been overlooked, as the

37

refundable earned income tax credit (EITC) benefits these workers and the rate of that credit would be raised from 10 percent to 12 percent and would be phased out of a higher income level than is true now. Critics of the social security tax credit note that the EITC does not benefit single workers or couples without children and, in their eyes, it remains regressive.

Opponents of the administration's tax cut proposal deny that the social security tax credit will reduce inflation significantly or increase employment substantially. First, they note that approximately two-thirds of the tax credit benefits will flow to individuals rather than to businesses and that this portion of the cut will not reduce employer costs, but rather most of its benefits will be spent by the taxpayers on consumption items, and such spending will add to inflationary pressures. There is no assurance either, according to critics of the credit, that employers will pass on reduced employment costs in lower prices to consumers. They may choose to use these funds to pay their workers higher wages in the present inflationary times and thus may add still more strength to inflationary pressures. Claims that tax savings from increased employment, due to the credit for employers, will partly offset the cost of the credits are, according to opponents, theoretical and tenuous, for many factors influence the unemployment rate, and employers are not likely to hire more workers if increased investment stimulated by other features of the tax program, such as depreciation reform, permit them to accomplish as much or more production with less labor cost per unit. Also, employers may prefer to pay experienced workers more money to retain their services rather than hire marginally productive new workers. Proponents claim that if, on the other hand, some employers do hire more workers, this action is likely to reduce the capital intensity of the economy. Labor and capital are two of the principal factors influencing production. Hiring more workers because the social security "labor" tax on employers is eased by the tax credit will, according to opponents of the credit, decrease the relative capital intensity of the production process over the long term as labor is substituted for capital. This, according to critics, runs counter to the notion of the tax cut program as an aid to reindustrialization and improved productivity per laborer.[118]

Advocates of the social security tax credit insist that any loss in the ratio of capital intensity will be slight and claim their data on probable increased employment are projected from past experience.

Targeted Individual Tax Cuts versus Across-the-Board Cuts. The contrast between the Republican tax cut proposal and that of the administration raises the issue of whether it is preferable to cut marginal tax rates or to target individual income tax cuts toward other features of the tax system and to avoid cutting marginal tax rates. The Republican proposal would cut individual tax rates across-the-board at a cost of $34.2 billion in fiscal 1982 per table 5, while the administration would provide individuals with a tax credit of 8 percent of their social security contributions, would provide a marriage penalty deduction, and would increase the earned income tax credit at a cost of about $19 billion in fiscal 1982, if we assume that two-thirds of the benefit of the social security tax credit will flow to workers and one-third to employers. (See table 7.) The Senate Finance Committee proposal follows both strategies. It would cut marginal tax rates at a fiscal 1982 cost of $14.3 billion and would increase the personal exemption, provide a marriage tax deduction, raise the zero bracket amount, and increase the EITC at an additional cost of $10.5 billion in fiscal 1982. In addition, individuals would benefit from a portion of the $2.7 billion reduction in the capital gains taxes that also benefits businesses. (See table 6.) The marriage penalty tax adjustment is a one-of-a-kind tax cut that may be supported by many of those who generally prefer across-the-board tax cuts for their macroeconomic effects. (The particulars of the marriage penalty tax adjustment and the increased EITC will be discussed later.) This subsection will focus directly on the relative merits of targeted individual tax cuts versus across-the-board cuts. The cost of the three tax cuts is not determinative of whether tax cuts should be targeted or across-the-board, for targeted cuts could be made quite as large as the proposed across-the-board tax cuts. When there is limited room in the budget for tax cuts, however, a clear-cut choice may be required if the desired effects of a tax cut are to be achieved.

Advocates of targeting tax cuts to the exclusion of across-the-board cuts contend that targeting enables the government to come to grips with problems of equity and efficiency and to promote macroeconomic goals. Targeting, proponents claim, helps rid the tax system of its more egregious distortions and inequities. For example, the marriage penalty would be substantially alleviated by the administration's proposal at a cost of $5.2 billion in fiscal 1982. An across-the-board tax cut, on the other hand, would reduce the amount of the penalty but it could not eliminate the penalty. Targeting tax relief for those most in need of relief increases the equity of the tax system, according to advocates of targeting. A general cut in individual tax rates under the Republican proposal, it is claimed, would average $2,170 for a family of four in the $100,000-a-year income bracket but only $150 for a family earning $17,500. Thus the general tax cut would do little to offset the coming increases in social security taxes for most low- and moderate-income families. Administration spokesmen insist that their plan of targeted cuts would increase the progressivity and equity of the tax system.[119]

Advocates of selective adjustments in the tax system rather than general rate cuts also maintain that targeted cuts are more likely to advance macroeconomic policy goals. Thus, for reasons outlined under "Tax Credit for Social Security Payroll Taxes," they argue that the social security tax credit will reduce inflationary pressures in the economy and will advance a major goal of the administration. This approach yields more "bang for the buck," more results per dollar of cost in achieving these goals, according to proponents. An across-the-board tax cut, on the other hand, would be quite inflationary, according to administration spokesmen, who claim that such a cut would do little to increase aggregate supply in the economy. According to some, it looks little different from old-fashioned pump-priming. The quick effects would be to put money in people's pockets. Would people use that money as supply-siders hope—save it or invest it, or lend it to the government to replace lost taxes? Critics of the plans to cut individual tax rates feel the change in the individual saving rate in response to lower tax rates would be quite small.[120] "Supply-side wishes would be quickly swamped by demand-side facts."[121]

On the other hand, these critics believe that such a tax cut would stimulate demand significantly. Output would increase, in this view, at the price of accelerating inflation. Walter Heller, chairman of the Council of Economic Advisers under President Kennedy, in June 1978 compared the Kemp-Roth proposal for individual tax cuts of 30 percent over three years with the individual tax rate cut of 1964 that pumped $12 billion into the economy (the equivalent of $35–40 billion in today's dollars). In his view, the greater part of "the success of the 'great tax cut' came, as expected, from the stimulus to *demand*."[122] This stimulus was desirable at that time, Heller says, because the economy had low industrial operating rates, slack in labor and product markets, and an inflation rate of 1.2 percent. Demand was stimulated with little inflation. Now, however, instead of the large increase in aggregate supply and the relatively small increase in aggregate demand that the proponents of the bill predict, skeptics claim that the actual response would be just the opposite and that it would lead to another round of roaring inflation.

Critics also claim that a general cut in individual tax rates does not address some of the important long-term problems facing us. Although almost everyone would like to reduce marginal tax rates on personal income, critics argue that a tax cut should not be "used up" on an item of low priority. Chairman Schultze of the Council of Economic Advisers states that "It is absolutely essential to the long-run health of our economy that when tax burdens are reduced we put additional dollars back into the private economy in a way which accomplishes long-term structural objectives."[123] These general objectives are to provide for greater economic growth in the future, higher productivity, and expanded supply. The commonly accepted methods for doing this are to utilize more capital, labor, and natural resources without stretching the availability of these inputs to their limits. Also, innovations and discoveries can provide capital and other resources at lower costs than before.

Many economists believe that general cuts in individual tax rates are not an effective way to stimulate such activity. In the words of Treasury Secretary G. William Miller, "Tax cuts designed simply for fiscal stimulus do little to enhance the economy's potential to produce goods and services."[124] Critics of general tax cuts reason that even if government spending is reduced by the full amount that taxes are cut, if all savings are consumed there is no change in investment, which is the major determinant of long-term growth. Thus, in this view, the benefits of the tax cut will be transitory and it may reignite inflation as well. Critics insist that before proponents of such a tax cut claim that it will address long-term needs, they must be certain that the tax cut would differ from others like it and that it would spur investment.

Advocates of general reduction in the marginal tax rate for individual taxpayers contend that across-the-board cuts are required to offset the effect of inflation in pushing taxpayers into higher and higher tax brackets, even though their real income—that is, the value of their income in purchasing power—may be less. Targeted cuts such as those proposed by the administration do not offset the effect of inflation and indeed do not fully offset the increases in the payroll tax that have been voted by the Congress. Thus the vast majority of our long-suffering taxpayers simply do not obtain relief from the effects of inflation under the administration's proposal. Although relief under the administration's targeted cuts is concentrated on those earning less than $10,000 a year, the administration's proposal does not fully offset the burden of increased payroll taxes, not to mention the inflation-induced burden of increased income taxes for the auto worker or industrial worker who earns $25,000 a year but falls further and further behind economically because of greater and greater taxes.[125]

40

Representative Clarence J. Brown (R-Ohio) points out that the average 1981 tax reduction on individual returns would be $63 under the administration's proposal, $268 under the Senate Finance Committee proposal, and $315 under the Republican tax cut proposal. He claims the average taxpayer will face a $335 increase in federal taxes in 1981, including inflation-induced increases and social security payroll tax increases, and only the Republican tax cut plan comes close to offsetting these increases for the average taxpayer. Advocates of marginal tax rate reductions reject the claim of greater equity in the administration's targeted tax cut plan. (See their arguments in the subsection "Tax Credit for Social Security Payroll Taxes.") Even if the administration were to cut average taxes by as much as the Republican plan, but in the pattern of the administration's plan, it is claimed that this action would not provide a fair return of taxes paid. Rather, the administration's proposal would take income away from those who earn more than $10,000 a year—and who pay almost all federal income taxes—and would transfer that income to those who pay very few taxes. Thus most taxpayers earning more than $10,000 a year would be better off without any tax cut, according to critics, than they would be with the administration's proposal. Advocates of marginal tax rate cuts cite an Internal Revenue Service survey showing that those with incomes under $10,000 whose returns were processed by July 31, 1980, paid only 4.4 percent of the taxes represented in those returns. Those who filed tax returns on incomes between $10,000 and $15,000 paid only 8 percent of the taxes, but taxpayers with incomes in excess of $15,000 paid 87.5 percent of the taxes. The real need, according to Charls Walker, is to reduce the "crushing middle-class tax burden."[126] Cutting marginal tax rates is fair, according to advocates, for the benefits of the tax cut are directly proportional to the amount of taxes these persons contribute, whether they are in high tax brackets or low brackets.

High marginal tax rates are causing serious distortions and disincentives in the economy, according to those who favor cutting these rates. The marginal rate is important in economic decision making because a person evaluating the worth of additional work or a better-paying job will consider the tax rate that is applicable to the additional or marginal earnings and not the average tax rate. When marginal tax rates reach a high level, income-earning activities are discouraged and tax revenues are lower than they would be if there were lower marginal tax rates. Advocates of "supply-side" economics point out that as marginal tax rates increase, workers have less and less incentive to earn income. Thus tax shelters become more valuable, the underground economy flourishes, and leisure time is more appealing. Earned income credits, larger personal exemptions, and raising the zero bracket amount have little or no effect on marginal tax rates so that they have little effect on incentive, it is claimed; in addition, supply-side advocates maintain these tax changes will not produce a greater level of supply.[127] A reduction in tax rates—in particular, marginal tax rates—is said to do more than just increase individual disposable incomes: It alters relative prices, changing the trade-off between work and leisure, savings and consumption.[128] It is by modifying these "prices" that the supply-side economists believe that output will rise sharply after a decrease in the tax rates. It follows that "It is most important to cut *top* rates, where most discretionary income-switching occurs."[129] Senator Orrin G. Hatch (R-Utah) contends that

The [Senate] Finance Committee's bill seems to waste about $7 billion in essentially rebate-type handouts that do not really lower the marginal tax rates. These are the revenues allocated to increasing the personal exemption, the zero rate bracket amount, and earned income credit. If government spending is not cut by an offsetting amount, this part of the bill, then, would be inflationary.[130]

The crux of the supply-side argument is that major changes that make leisure and consumption significantly less favored by taxpayers will spur output and investment a great deal: "Perhaps the most important point about supply-side theory is that after incentives are changed, the future can no longer be projected as a continuation of the past. Those who express tax-rate reductions as revenue losses precisely fail to allow for this."[131] Proponents of general tax cuts insist that we need not accept all of the supply-side theory to agree that many of the inefficiencies and distortions in the economy can be eliminated by reducing tax rates. They point out that "The seeker of tax shelters bears a high cost for his activity. He must often accept a low before-tax rate of return [municipal bonds] or accept very high risk relative to the expected rate of return [oil well drilling]. In addition, huge fees must often be paid to syndicators, accountants, and lawyers."[132] Again, if tax rates are lowered, these options will become less attractive, and the less that the tax system distorts behavior, the fewer economic inefficiencies there will be.

A major concern of some proponents of a general tax cut is the growing conviction that the federal government has been allocating too much of the national income to itself, and that the time has come to reverse this policy.[133] In their view, the interventionist philosophy of government has created many of our troubles. An across-the-board tax cut, it is claimed, would reduce the role of the federal government in the economy and would stimulate greater effort in the private sector. These critics of government taxing and spending reject the notion that it is proper and necessary for the government to "target" its program to manage the direction of economic activity—that is, to determine where investments are made, what prices and wages are charged, what industries are to be supported. They favor a system in which government plays an essential but limited role, which it discharges in accord with constitutional processes, but in which decisions are predominantly made by private individuals and associations of private individuals acting within the limits set by competitive markets. In other words, resources should be allocated in a free marketplace without overbearing government intervention through either tax or regulatory policy.[134]

Reduction of the "Marriage Penalty." The "marriage tax" is a misnomer. There is no actual tax on the state of marriage, but a quirk in the structure of the individual income tax frequently causes the total tax of two earners to increase upon marriage. This happens because the first dollar of one spouse's income is taxed at the marginal rate of the other spouse's last dollar of income. The lower tax rates for married couples compared with those paid by single taxpayers are not always enough to offset this effect, and the marriage penalty is particularly pronounced when couples earn high incomes that are relatively equal in amount. (See table 8.) The potential for the marriage tax differential always existed in the tax structure, but it did not become a significant problem until 1969, when Congress determined that single

TABLE 8

Effect of Marriage on Present Law Tax Liability at Selected Income Levels and Earnings Splits between Husband and Wife[a]

Total Family Income ($)	Share of Lesser-Earning Spouse (percent)										
	0	5	10	15	20	25	30	35	40	45	50
5,000	−250	−210	−170	−133	−98	−63	−28	0	0	0	0
7,000	−378	−315	−252	−189	−126	−66	−10	46	98	147	168
10,000	−475	−370	−275	−180	−85	10	100	162	182	200	202
15,000	−710	−515	−328	−148	32	132	183	220	236	243	251
20,000	−1,092	−760	−460	−160	42	150	238	300	355	381	391
25,000	−1,505	−1,055	−630	−268	−30	160	310	447	535	594	611
30,000	−1,929	−1,334	−749	−334	−26	214	449	644	785	875	903
40,000	−2,801	−1,821	−939	−338	177	667	1,031	1,329	1,564	1,644	1,692
50,000	−3,344	−2,094	−1,094	−286	454	1,133	1,731	2,121	2,439	2,574	2,674
100,000	−3,464	−1,214	359	1,691	2,699	3,474	4,014	4,314	4,369	4,394	4,394

[a] Assumes that taxpayers have no dependents and do not itemize deductions. Marriage penalties would be smaller, and marriage bonuses larger, for itemizers. Marriage penalties are positive in table; marriage bonuses are negative.

Source: U.S. Congress, House of Representatives, Ways and Means Committee, Committee Print 96-56, *Explanation of Tax Restructuring Act of 1980,* April 10, 1980, p. 25.

taxpayers should pay no more than 120 percent of the tax paid by married couples at the same income level.[135] There had been a "tax on being single" in many cases before this change was made. Since 1969, rising incomes and greater labor force participation of wives have made the "marriage penalty" a substantial concern to many couples.

The proposals to deal with this problem advanced by the Senate Finance Committee and the Carter administration are identical except for a one-year transition period in the Senate bill in order to phase in the deduction. This reform would reduce marginal tax rates for the second earner's income by 10 percent. Another proposal that has substantial support would allow married couples the option of filing as if they were both single if this is to their advantage.[136]

The principal argument in favor of proposals to eliminate or ameliorate the marriage tax is that the marriage penalty is an inequity that should be corrected. Representative Millicent Fenwick (R-N.J.) complains that "our tax system shouldn't force people into cohabitation or divorce. It shouldn't penalize people who get married."[137] Many think that this part of the tax code has simply not kept up with social change. Representative Fenwick notes that "In 1950, only 18 percent of married women living with their husbands worked. That figure had increased to 48 percent by 1977."[138] More and more married women are encountering the marriage tax by entering the labor force. Senator Charles McC. Mathias, Jr. (R-Md.) claims that the marriage penalty affects all income levels and that a couple's tax bill can be as much as 63 percent higher because of the marriage tax.[139]

High marginal taxes for the second income of many married couples produces a work disincentive, especially when work-related costs such as expenses for child care, housekeeping services, and the like are figured in. Some observers insist that this is a case where the effective marginal tax rate is high, and reduction of that rate would provide great benefits at a relatively low cost. The Joint Committee on Taxation has estimated that 15 to 16 million couples would benefit from this tax cut of between $7 and $9 billion.[140]

Those opposing the tax law changes recommended by the Senate Finance Committee and the administration do not endorse the marriage tax in principle but insist that other inequities would be created by this particular change.

> As long as tax rates are progressive, some group of taxpayers will be shortchanged. It's either married couples with two incomes (as the law stands) or married couples with one income (as the law would be if Mathias-Fenwick prevails [see note 136]) or single people (if all married couples were allowed to split the family income).[141]

If tax rates are progressive, then there must be a "marriage tax," a "single's tax," or differences in taxes paid by equal-income couples, or some combination of these. Thus, under current law, the married couple composed of a person earning significant income and another without income will always pay less total tax than before marriage, since they will gain the benefit of the lower tax rates for married couples. In general it is only when the spouse with the lower earnings earns more than 20–25 percent of the couple's income that the marriage "subsidy" created by the lower tax rate for married persons becomes the marriage "tax" caused by one use of the zero bracket amount. (See table 8.) But lowering the marginal tax rates for married couples would only increase the "single's tax."

44

The 10 percent deduction of the income of the spouse with the lower earnings would, it is asserted, create differences in the tax liabilities of couples earning the same total. This situation would arise where the spouses' incomes are more equally divided. The earnings of the spouse with the lower income would be higher, and the special deduction would be higher. It should be noted that this deduction is really a different type of proposal than the Fenwick-Mathias bill cited in note 136. While the Fenwick-Mathias bill would allow any couple paying a "marriage penalty" (but only those who do) to legally avoid it, the deduction for working couples under the administration's bill and under the Senate Finance Committee bill would allow a subtraction that could be more or less than the current marriage penalty. Some not currently paying the marriage penalty would have their taxes reduced because there is not a perfect correspondence between those couples earning two wages and those paying the marriage penalty (see table 8), and some would have a reduction greater than the penalty. At the same time, it is claimed, the deduction will undercompensate some other taxpayers.

Liberalizing the Earned Income Tax Credit. The Senate Finance Committee bill would increase the earned income tax credit (EITC) by raising the refundable credit from 10 percent of the first $5,000 of income to 11 percent and by phasing out the credit at a higher level of income than before. The administration would increase the rate of the EITC to 12 percent of the first $5,000 of earnings, and it would also phase down the credit at a higher level.[142]

The Senate Finance Committee and the administration advocate an increase in the EITC to provide relief from the scheduled social security tax increases for low-income families. The Senate Finance Committee increase would compensate for inflation since 1978.[143] The social security payroll tax is payable on the first dollar of labor income without deductions or exemptions, such as those in the income tax, and thus it hits the working poor especially hard. The original intent of the EITC was to refund the social security payroll tax to those with low incomes and thus to remove work disincentives for welfare families. Refundability provides relief to low-income persons whose incomes are so low that they have no income taxes against which they can offset the tax credit. For these reasons the EITC has been labeled one of the five major welfare programs in the United States, although it will account for only about 6.6 percent of federal welfare costs in fiscal 1980.[144] Some refer to the EITC as one of the most significant steps to be taken by the federal government in recent years to relieve the tax burdens of the poor.[145] Advocates of increasing the EITC note that administrative costs are low and that the distribution of benefits is almost automatic. Currently some 6 million families benefit from the EITC, and the average benefit is about $310 per family per year.[146]

Critics of the EITC argue that although it may provide some families with work incentives, it provides many more families with work disincentives. Under the current formula, for example, an individual earning less than $5,000 who is without an appreciable amount of other income receives an additional $1 of credit for every $10 earned. This is an effective 10 percent labor income subsidy to such workers. As the credit is phased out in the $6,000–10,000 range, however, $1.25 of the EITC is lost for every $10 increase in earned income. Hence there is a negative work subsidy of 12.5 percent in this income range. The Senate Finance Committee bill would increase this negative subsidy rate to 13.75 percent, and the administration bill would increase it to 15 percent. When explicit taxes—federal and state personal income taxes and the payroll tax—are added to this implicit tax, the effective marginal rate can rise beyond 30 percent, a tax rate not equaled by other taxpayers until their wages rise well over the median income level.[147] Some 64 percent of those receiving the EITC were in the phase-out range at last count and critics believe that on balance the net effect of the EITC is to increase disincentives to work.[148]

Another criticism of the EITC is that it fails to meet the minimum criteria of a good welfare program because of its limited coverage, its inverse relation to need, its disregard of family size, and its tendency to undermine family structures.[149] Because the credit is limited to families who have dependent children, singles and families without dependent children do not receive any benefits.

Those earning more, up to $5,000 under current law, receive more. A family with $5,000 of income receives $500, but a family with income of $3,000 receives only a $300 credit. Since need is generally measured by income, the EITC is said to contradict the principle of aiding those who have the greatest need. The third objection noted is that the EITC does not vary with family size, and a small family receives the same credit as a larger family with the same income. Critics also claim the EITC may encourage families to separate. A married couple with two $5,000 salaries would be ineligible for the EITC. However, if the family splits and each parent takes a child, each parent could claim a $500 EITC. Some critics of the EITC object to general revenue financing of part of the cost of social security through the refundability of the EITC for reasons stated in the section "Refundability of the Social Security Credit." Also, social security beneficiaries receive benefits "free" to the extent that the EITC offsets their payroll taxes and thus breaks the tie to a contributory system for some beneficiaries.

On the other side, it is argued that general revenue funding is appropriate to pay the welfare portion of social security benefits stemming from the weighted benefit formula, dependent's benefits, and the minimum benefit. The payroll tax would not be an acceptable means of financing social security for low-income families, according to some, if the EITC did not protect low-income families.[150]

NOTES TO TEXT

1 The Republican proposal adopts most of the first-year changes proposed in the Kemp-Roth bill. The Kemp-Roth bill, however, would cut personal taxes by a like amount in each of two additional years, reducing marginal tax rates by an aggregate of about 30 percent in the third year. Thereafter the Kemp-Roth plan would index all taxable income brackets, personal exemptions, standard deductions, and depreciation allowances to the GNP deflator to offset the effect of inflation on the income tax system. Several sponsors of the Republican proposal favor the additional tax cuts proposed in the Kemp-Roth bill, but they do not insist on inclusion of those cuts in the instant proposal in order to present a united front to aid adoption of tax cut legislation in the current Congress. A number of lawmakers agree with Governor Reagan that such tax cuts must be coupled with substantial reductions in the rate of growth of government spending, though spending restrictions are not an explicit part of the Republican proposal.

2 This proposal, titled the Capital Cost Recovery Act, was introduced by Representatives James R. Jones (D-Okla.) and Barber B. Conable, Jr. (R-N.Y.) as H.R. 4646 and by Senators Gaylord Nelson (D-Wis.), Lloyd M. Bentsen (D-Tex.), Bob Packwood (R-Oreg.), and John H. Chafee (R-R.I.) as S. 1435.

3 Depreciation is the process by which the cost of an asset is allocated under current law to the years of its anticipated useful life. Tax authorities contend that writing off the cost of an asset in the year of its acquisition (expensing) would overstate true costs in the first year and understate costs in future years. The method of depreciation employed to allocate asset costs affects the level of profits and of taxes for the years of an asset's useful life.

4 This and other concepts and the arguments for and against the 10-5-3 proposal are examined in greater detail in *The Capital Cost Recovery Act Proposal*, Legislative Analysis No. 17 (Washington, D.C.: The American Enterprise Institute, 1980).

5 This depreciation reform proposal was previously introduced by Senator Lloyd M. Bentsen (D-Tex.) as S. 3040.

6 Depreciation may be at 200, 150, or 100 percent of the straight-line rate. This rate fixes annual depreciation at the total amount depreciable multiplied by $(1/n)$, where n is the life in years of the asset. The taxpayer can make an annual election of the rate to be employed.

7 Representative Richard A. Gephardt (D-Mo.) and Senator Bill Bradley (D-N.J.) previously introduced H.R. 7046 and S. 2920, respectively, to provide a refundable tax credit similar in most respects to the administration's proposal.

8 U.S. Congressional Budget Office, *An Analysis of the Roth-Kemp Tax Cut Proposal,* 1978, pp. 9–11.

9 Quoted in James R. Dickenson, "Reagan Backs Big Cuts for Biggest Taxpayers," *Washington Star,* June 1, 1980, p. A-3.

10 U.S. Congress, Joint Economic Committee, *Hearings on Special Study of Economic Change* (hereafter *Economic Change Hearings*) 96th Congress, 1st session, July 27,

1979, p. 84, statement of Rudolph Penner, director of tax policy studies at the American Enterprise Institute.

[11] "Inflation: High Inflation, Taxes Cause Real Income Levels to Decline," *Bureau of National Affairs, Daily Report for Executives* (hereafter *BNA DER*), September 24, 1980, p. G-4; "Inflation: Pay Hike Equal to Inflation Rate Won't Stop Income Loss, Tax Group Says," *BNA DER*, June 27, 1980, p. G-2.

[12] *Congressional Record,* vol. 126 (June 25, 1980), p. 8208.

[13] Walter W. Heller, "Piercing the Budgetary Fog," *Wall Street Journal,* June 30, 1980, p. 14.

[14] *Economic Change Hearings,* p. 88, table 1, statement of George F. Break, professor of economics, University of California at Berkeley; ibid., p. 88, statement of Penner; James L. Rowe, Jr., "Inflation's Illusions: Also Hitting Business," *Washington Post,* August 28, 1980, p. D-1; James A. Tatom and James E. Turley, "Inflation and Taxes: Disincentives for Capital Formation," *St. Louis Federal Reserve Board Review,* vol. 60 (January 1978), pp. 2, 4–5.

[15] *Economic Change Hearings,* p. 87, statement of Penner.

[16] Martin Feldstein and Lawrence Summers, "Inflation and the Taxation of Capital Income in the Corporate Sector," *National Tax Journal,* vol. 32 (December 1979), pp. 445–46, 448, 463, 468. If one assumption relied upon by Feldstein and Summers is disregarded because of uncertainty, increased taxes due to inflation would be $14.06 billion rather than $26.1 billion. See *The Capital Cost Recovery Act Proposal,* pp. 8–9.

[17] U.S. Department of Commerce, *Survey of Current Business,* September 1978, p. 47.

[18] *The Capital Cost Recovery Act Proposal,* pp. 2–3; U.S. Congress, Senate, Committee on Finance, Subcommittee on Taxation and Debt Management, *Hearings on Capital Cost Recovery,* 96th Congress, 1st session, October 22, 1979, p. 19, table 8, prepared statement of George A. Strichman, Committee for Effective Capital Recovery.

[19] "The Road to Budget Balance," in Don Ritter, "In Support of Tax Reductions," *Congressional Record,* vol. 126 (August 26, 1980), pp. E 4010, E 4011. Increased federal tax growth includes inflation's effect on personal and corporate taxes, the social security tax increases required by the 1977 Social Security Act amendments, the windfall profits tax, and so forth. Alan Greenspan, a former chairman of the Council of Economic Advisers, also refers to a $86 billion increase in the federal tax burden in fiscal 1981. "Tax Cuts: Heller, Greenspan Urge Tax Action Soon to Aid Recovery," *BNA DER,* July 22, 1980, p. G-8. Representative John H. Rousselot (R-Calif.) estimated the 1981 federal tax increase at between $95 billion and $100 billion, the most massive in history and likely to require the average family of four to pay approximately $500 more in taxes in 1981 than in 1980. Representative Rousselot contends that taxes will then be at the highest level in history, higher than levels during World War II and during the Korean War, and higher than the Vietnam surcharge, *Congressional Record,* vol. 126 (June 26, 1980), pp. H 5765–H 5769. Business Council economists estimate the federal tax increase for 1981 at $100 billion. "Tax Cuts: GE's Jones Urges $36 Billion Tax Package Effective January 1, 1981," *BNA DER,* June 30, 1980, p. LL-1. Representative W. Henson Moore (R-La.) estimates that federal receipts will climb to $92 billion in fiscal 1981 and that $39 billion of this amount will be raised by new net revenue raising measures initiated by the current administration. *Congressional Record,* vol. 126 (June 26, 1980), p. H 5767.

[20] "Tax Policy: New 'Tax Index' Shows Rise in Taxes Outpaces Prices, Production," *BNA DER*, May 28, 1980, p. G-7.

[21] U.S. Congress, Joint Economic Committee, *Hearings on the Underground Economy*, 96th Congress, 1st session, November 15, 1979, pp. 2–14, statement of Jerome Kurtz, commissioner of internal revenue; ibid., pp. 21-35, statement of Gutmann; "Remarks of Rep. Al Ullman on the 'Tax Restructuring Act of 1980,'" *BNA DER*, April 3, 1980, p. J-1; "The Underground Economy," *U.S. News & World Report*, October 22, 1979, p. 46. The IRS believes that farmers fail to report 30 percent of their income, while the Census Bureau estimates that 52 percent of farm income remains unrecorded. The Labor Department believes that 25 percent of the illegal aliens in this country work "off-the-books." The IRS believes that the self-employed report only 60 percent of their income. The House Wednesday Group, *Backgrounder on the Underground Economy*, August 27, 1980, p. 2.

[22] See, for example, *Economic Change Hearings*, p. 91, statement of Penner.

[23] Marginal tax rates were cut 5 percent per year in Puerto Rico over a three-year period. Tax revenues, it is claimed, have increased by 13.5 percent. Tom Bethell, "What Kemp-Roth Would Really Do," *Washington Post*, October 1, 1980, p. A-17.

[24] Council of Economic Advisers, *Economic Indicators*, September 1980, pp. 17–18.

[25] Ibid., pp. 3, 12.

[26] "The Road to Budget Balance," p. E 4011.

[27] Executive Office of the President, *Economic Report of the President, 1980*, pp. 50, 205.

[28] Executive Office of the President, *The Budget of the U.S. Government, Fiscal Year 1981*, p. 42.

[29] Walter W. Heller, "Piercing the Budgetary Fog," *Congressional Record*, vol. 126 (July 2, 1980), p. S 9372. Heller's figures use National Income Account definitions.

[30] Ibid.

[31] "An Economic Dream in Peril," *Newsweek*, September 8, 1980, pp. 50, 52; "The U.S. Productivity Crisis," *Newsweek*, September 8, 1980, pp. 53, 54; "The Basics in Trouble," *Newsweek*, September 8, 1980, pp. 55, 58; "Productivity: Two Experts Cross Swords," *Newsweek*, September 8, 1980, pp. 67–69, quoting Nobel laureates in economics Paul A. Samuelson and Milton Friedman; Gary Hart, "S. 3060, A Bill to Exempt from Income Tax the Capital Gain from the First Resale of New Capacity Stock," *Congressional Record*, vol. 126 (August 22, 1980), pp. S 11425–S 11427; "Remarks of Sen. Lloyd Bentsen (D-Tex.) on Introduction of the 'Investment Tax Act of 1980,'" *BNA DER*, August 19, 1980, p. J-1; Harrison H. Schmitt, "Savings and Investment Incentives Act of 1980," *Congressional Record*, vol. 126 (July 31, 1980), pp. S 10473–S 10486; Ritter, "In Support of Tax Reductions," p. E 4011; Feldstein and Summers, "Inflation and the Taxation of Capital Income," p. 468; U.S. Congress, House of Representatives, Committee on Small Business, *Hearings on Small Business, Productivity, Innovation, and Taxation*, 96th Congress, 1st session, October 17, 1979, pp. 18–28, statement of Richard L. Boyce, senior economist, Council on Wage and Price Stability.

[32] *Economic Change Hearings*, p. 81, statement of Break.

[33] "Tax Policy: Administration Officials Say Business Would Get Bigger Share of 1981 Tax Cut," *BNA DER*, June 24, 1980, p. LL-1; Senate and House Committees on the Budget, *The Economic Outlook at Midyear 1980*, July 1980, p. 62. The General Accounting Office notes that when there is a deficit, private savers transfer funds to the government. Reducing the deficit reduces the size of the transfer, and thus releases funds for private capital formation. "This is probably the most direct and effective means available for the Federal Government to increase total saving and capital formation." U.S. General Accounting Office, *An Analytical Framework for Federal Policies and Programs Influencing Capital Formation in the United States*, September 23, 1980, pp. 53, 79.

[34] See table 6 in *The Capital Cost Recovery Act Proposal*, p. 23.

[35] Caroline Atkinson, "Senate Unit Hastens Tax Cuts," *Washington Post*, August 20, 1980, p. A-10.

[36] See the Joint Committee on Taxation staff summary of additional spending proposals in the administration's plan in "JCT Staff Summary of Administration's Proposals," *BNA DER*, September 4, 1980, pp. J-1–J-2.

[37] Rudolph G. Penner, "The Future Growth of Government Budgets," in William Fellner, ed., *Contemporary Economic Problems* (Washington, D.C.: American Enterprise Institute, 1980), pp. 118–19.

[38] Executive Office of the President, *Mid-Session Review of the 1981 Budget*, July 21, 1980, p. 3.

[39] Rudolph G. Penner, "Tax Policies in the 1980s," *The AEI Economist*, August 1980, p. 6.

[40] "Does the Economy Need a Big Tax Cut?" *The American Legion*, vol. 109 (July 1980), p. 10.

[41] "Economic Policy," *BNA DER*, August 25, 1980, p. LL-1. Governor Reagan, for example, announced on September 9, 1980, spending cuts increasing from 2 percent in 1981 to 7 percent in 1985 with a goal of 3 percent cuts in 1981 increasing to 10 percent by 1984. "Fact Sheet on Republican Presidential Candidate Ronald Reagan's Economic Program," *BNA DER*, September 9, 1980, pp. X-1, X-3. He would also accept the less expensive depreciation reform contained in the Senate Finance Committee bill. Art Pine, "Reagan Changes Leave Some Questions," *Washington Post*, September 10, 1980, p. E-1.

[42] Roger W. Jepsen, "The Case for a Tax Cut Now," *Congressional Record*, vol. 126 (September 29, 1980), p. S 13730; *Congressional Record*, vol. 126 (June 26, 1980), p. H 5771, statement of Representative Rhodes; Robert Dole, "Taxflation and Tax Abatement," *Congressional Record*, vol. 126 (August 1, 1980), p. S 1058; Frank N. Wilner, "Of Tax Cuts and Fiscal Trickery," *Washington Star*, July 12, 1980, p. A-11.

[43] "Economic Analysis: Supply Side Economics Provides New Rationale for Tax Reduction," *BNA DER*, September 7, 1979, pp. P-2–P-3; Robert W. Merry, "Senate Panel Disputes Miller on Tax Cut," *Wall Street Journal*, July 24, 1980, p. 10; William V. Roth, Jr., "Reagan-Kemp-Roth," *Congressional Record*, vol. 126 (September 30, 1980), p. S 14156; Jepsen "The Case for a Tax Cut Now," pp. S 13728, S 13730; and see U.S. Congress, Joint Economic Committee, *Hearings on Issues of Federal Finance*, July 25, 27, 1979, p. 109, statement of Penner. Evans Econometrics estimated that the Kemp-Roth bill, a more expensive package than the Republican tax cut proposal, would

lower projected revenues by $152 billion in 1985, but that added revenues from stronger growth would cut the net loss in that year to $87 billion. Ibid., p. S 13730. The 40 percent "rule of thumb" works as follows: historically tax cuts increase GNP by slightly less than twice the size of the initial revenue loss. Since federal revenues are about 20 percent of GNP, the increase in federal receipts is about (0.20 × 20 = 0.40) or 40 percent.

44 *Hearings on Capital Cost Recovery,* September 21–22, 1979, statement of G. William Miller, p. 4. Allen Sinai of Data Resources, Inc., estimated that the feedback effect of the 10-5-3 plan would amount to 40 percent. Allen Sinai, *Economic Impacts of Accelerated Capital Cost Recovery* (Washington, D.C.: Bureau of National Affairs, Inc., 1979), p. J-4, fn. 7.

45 "Capital Gains: Securities Industry Pushes for Further Reductions in Tax," *BNA DER,* August 1, 1980, pp. K-1, K-3; Steven D. Symms, "The Venture and Equity Capital Revitalization Act of 1980," *Congressional Record,* vol. 126 (August 22, 1980), pp. E 3977-E 3978.

46 The Tax Cut Dilemma," *Washington Post,* July 26, 1980, p. A-18; "Supply-Side Economics: Idea Whose Time Has Not Come," *Washington Post,* August 17, 1980, p. F-5; "Political Campaigns Draw Lines over Tax Cuts," *Congressional Quarterly,* vol. 38 (August 2, 1980), pp. 2155–56; Herbert Stein, "Curriculum for Economics 1981," *The AEI Economist,* June 1980, p. 8. (Stein notes that "Supply-side measures are unlikely to be effective quickly enough to make a major contribution to solving the inflation problem within the time in which it must be solved.")

47 Economic Policy: Fed Chairman Opposes Both Carter and Reagan Tax-Cut Plans," *BNA DER,* September 10, 1980, pp. LL-1–LL-2; Jonathan Fuerbringer, "U.S. Business Leaders Split on Tax Cut," *Washington Star,* July 26, 1980, p. B-5 (Herbert Stein cited as opposing any tax cut because it might send out a signal that the government will not stick with its anti-inflation effort long enough to succeed); David Wood, "Burns Calls GOP Tax Move 'Inflationary, Premature,' " *Washington Star,* July 8, 1980, p. A-4 (Arthur Burns, former chairman of the Federal Reserve Board, notes that we would be attacking a short-term problem—unemployment—when we should be worrying about the long-term problem of inflation; a deliberate enlargement of the federal deficit will continue to nourish the forces of inflation); Jane Bryant Quinn, "Tax Cuts Up Close," *Newsweek,* vol. 96 (September 29, 1980), p. 71.

48 "Two for the Tax Cut Seesaw," *Washington Post,* July 7, 1980, p. A-14. According to one recent study, the Federal Reserve Board permits a more rapid rate of growth in the money supply in order to reduce the upward pressure that a greater government debt, that is induced by heavy spending and deficits, places on interest rates, and this accommodative policy adds to the rate of inflation. Mickey Levy, "Factors Affecting Monetary Policy in an Era of Inflation," paper presented at the 50th annual convention of the Southern Economic Association, Washington, D.C., November 6, 1980.

49 "Economic Policy: Kahn Attacks Reagan on Tax Cut Proposal," *BNA DER,* September 12, 1980, p. LL-1. To the same effect, see Judith Miller, "Miller Sees Dangers in Tax Cut," *New York Times,* July 23, 1980, p. D-17 (quoting Treasury Secretary Miller), and "Tax Cuts: Finance Does the Impossible," *BNA DER,* August 22, 1980, p. K-1 (citing the statement of Senator Bob Packwood [R-Oreg.] that if the Senate Finance Committee bill becomes law the country may exchange $1 in lower taxes for $2 in higher prices and at the same time jeopardize jobs and economic security).

[50] *Congressional Record*, vol. 126 (June 26, 1980), pp. S 8405–S 8406.

[51] "Tax Cuts: Former Fed Chief Burns Urges Delay in Tax-Cut Legislation," *BNA DER*, July 7, 1980, pp. AA-3–AA-4. The Congressional Budget Office estimated in 1978 that the Kemp-Roth tax cut proposal, which would cut personal taxes by 30 percent in three stages rather than by 10 percent as in the Republican proposal, would add 2.7 points to the inflation rate after its fifth year of enactment. Congressional Budget Office, *An Analysis of the Roth-Kemp Tax Cut Proposal*, p. 45 (the inflation rate referred to is that measured by the Consumer Price Index). The economy was stronger when this projection was made and thus more vulnerable to an increase in inflation.

[52] "U.S. Budget: Administration Officials Plug Carter's Economic Plans, Attack GOP Tax Cuts," *BNA DER*, September 8, 1980, pp. LL-1, LL-2.

[53] "Economic Outlook: Chamber of Commerce Attacks Administration Economic Program," *BNA DER*, August 29, 1980, p. LL-1; Orrin G. Hatch, "Dawdling with Incentives," *Congressional Record*, vol. 126 (September 4, 1980), p. S 12095. Representative Kemp refers to the administration's tax cut proposal as the sort of demand-stimulus program that the bipartisan Joint Economic Committee does not favor. Jack Kemp, "What Does President Carter Have Against the U.S. Economy?" *Congressional Record*, vol. 126 (August 28, 1980), p. H 8128.

[54] Robert Dole, "The Tax Reduction–Job Creation Act," *Congressional Record*, vol. 126 (June 25, 1980), p. S 8207.

[55] GAO, *An Analytical Framework*, p. 2; "Economic Outlook: Three Private Economists Support Large Tax Cuts to Bolster Growth," *BNA DER*, July 27, 1978, pp. G-6–G-7.

[56] Orrin G. Hatch, "The Case for Supply-Side Economics," *Congressional Record*, vol. 126 (September 4, 1980), p. S 12095; Jepsen, "The Case for a Tax Cut Now," p. S 13730. For the effect of the 10-5-3 depreciation reform on international trade and the balance of payments, see *The Capital Cost Recovery Act Proposal*, pp. 18–19. In 1978, commenting on the possible effect of the more liberal Kemp-Roth plan on inflation, Representative Robert N. Giaimo (D-Conn.), chairman of the House Budget Committee, claimed that models showed that the Kemp-Roth plan would add 1–4 percent to the consumer price index by 1984. Jack Carlson, the then chief economist for the Chamber of Commerce of the United States, claimed Kemp-Roth would not be inflationary if spending growth were held to $38 billion in 1979 and 7 percent a year thereafter. "Tax Cuts: Giaimo calls Kemp-Roth Plan Inflationary," *BNA DER*, July 24, 1978, pp. G-4, G-5.

[57] *Congressional Record*, vol. 126 (August 18, 1980), p. S 11153; Merry, "Senate Panel Disputes Miller on Tax Cut," p. 10; "Tax Cuts: Finance Clears Measure with $39 Billion Calendar Year 1981 Price Tag," *BNA DER*, August 21, 1980, p. G-4.

[58] "Economic Policy: JEC Report Urges $25 Billion Supply Side Tax Cut," *BNA DER*, February 28, 1980, p. LL-1; "Tax Plan Favors Business Incentives," *Washington Post*, August 29, 1980, pp. A-1, A-9; John M. Berry, "Carter Tax Plan: A Gamble with Voters," *Washington Post*, August 30, 1980, p. C-8.

[59] William V. Roth, Jr., "The Roth-Kemp Tax Cuts," *Christian Science Monitor*, September 27, 1978; *Congressional Record*, vol. 126 (June 26, 1980), p. H 5763 (statement of Representative Conable); "Tax Cuts: Despite Some Resistance, GOP Plan May Make Tax Bill This Year Inevitable," *BNA DER*, July 3, 1980, p. K-1 (statement of Taub); Paul Craig Roberts, "Carter's Tax Package," *Wall Street Journal*, September 25, 1980.

[60] "President's Comments on Economy," *Washington Star*, August 29, 1980, p. A-6.

[61] U.S. Congress, House of Representatives, Committee on Ways and Means, *Hearings on the Advisability of a Tax Cut*, 96th Congress, 2d session, August 21, 1980, p. 2, statement of Carl E. Bagge; "Autos: Support Industries May Face $80 Billion in Retooling Costs to 1985," *BNA DER*, October 16, 1980, p. L-2.

[62] Ritter, "In Support of Tax Reductions," p. E 4011.

[63] CBO, *The Economic Outlook at Midyear 1980*, p. 63.

[64] "Carter Economic Plan: A Timely Melange," *Congressional Quarterly*, vol. 38 (August 30, 1980), p. 2563.

[65] Jepsen, "The Case for a Tax Cut Now," pp. S 13727–S 13729; Edgar K. Browning and William R. Johnson, *The Distribution of the Tax Burden* (Washington, D.C.: American Enterprise Institute, 1979), table 15, p. 64 (state and local sales and excise taxes average 3.5 percent), table 14, p. 63 (average taxpayer pays 1.4 percent in federal excise taxes), and table 16, p. 66 (average tax rate of 56.1 percent on capital income).

[66] Jepsen, "The Case for a Tax Cut Now," pp. S 13727–S 13729; William V. Roth, Jr., "Reagan-Roth-Kemp," pp. S 14155-S 14157; Hatch, "The Case for Supply-Side Economics," pp. S 12093–S 12095. Representative Thomas B. Evans, Jr. (R-Del.), claims that "Increasing disincentives to work and produce by raising taxes to virtually unprecedented levels weakens the capacity of our economy to produce the volume of goods and services needed to meet consumer demand. . . . A tax cut oriented towards the supply side of our economy will encourage business to invest more capital in more modern means of production, as well as provide individuals with an incentive to work more productively." *Congressional Record*, vol. 126 (June 26, 1980), p. H 5770.

[67] "U.S. Budget: Administration Officials Plug Carter's Economic Plans, Attack GOP Tax Cuts," pp. L-1, LL-2; "Economic Policy: Chamber Unveils Plan to Rebuild America's Industrial Base," *BNA DER*, September 3, 1980, p. LL-1; Otto Eckstein, a former chairman of the Council of Economic Advisers and president of Data Resources, Inc., employed a supply-side model in estimating that raising the business investment credit from 10 to 12.7 percent and accelerating the depreciation of business equipment by four years would produce a 15.6 percent increase in business fixed investment and a 7.2 percent increase in the capital stock by the end of the decade. "Economic Policy: JEC Report Urges $25 Billion Supply Side Tax Cut," p. LL-1; "The Huge Stakes in 10-5-3 Depreciation," *Business Week*, October 1, 1979, pp. 124–25.

[68] Robert E. Hall and Dale W. Jorgenson, "Tax Policy and Investment Behavior," *American Economic Review*, vol. 57 (June 1967), p. 414; and see Robert E. Hall and Dale W. Jorgenson, "Application of the Theory of Optimum Capital Accumulation," in Gary Fromm, ed., *Tax Incentives and Capital Spending* (Washington, D.C.: The Brookings Institution, 1971), p. 9. Some claim that personal saving increased $10 billion and investment spending increased by nearly $38 billion between 1961 and 1965 largely as a result of the Kennedy tax cuts. James Green, "Kemp-Roth Revives an Earlier Success," *Atlanta Constitution*, August 31, 1980.

[69] U.S. Congress, Senate, Committee on Finance, Subcommittee on Taxation and Debt Management, *Hearings on Incentives for Economic Growth*, 95th Congress, 1st session, June 15, 1977, statement of Gramley, p. 2.

[70] "Pressing a Capital Idea," *Time*, June 4, 1979, p. 40.

[71] U.S. Congress, Senate, Committee on Finance, Subcommittee on Taxation and Debt Management, *Hearings on Capital Formation,* 95th Congress, 1st session, June 15, 1977, statement of Laurence N. Woodworth, assistant secretary of the treasury for tax policy, p. 1; "Digest of GAO Report on 'Investment Tax Credit,'" *BNA DER,* May 16, 1978, p. J-3.

[72] Robert J. Samuelson, "Investment Incentives: Politics May Come First," *Washington Post,* September 16, 1980, p. E-1, citing economist Edward F. Denison; Hobart Rowen, "Brookings Calls '70s 'The Most Disappointing,'" *Washington Post,* August 21, 1980, pp. D-1–D-2; "Tax Cuts: Senate Democratic Task Force Lists Options for Tax Cut Recommendation," *BNA DER,* July 23, 1980, pp. G-1, J-2; "Economic Policy: Brookings Papers Attack Supply-Side Rationale for Tax Reductions." *BNA DER,* August 20, 1980, pp. LL-4–LL-5.

[73] "Digest of GAO Report on 'Investment Tax Credit,'" p. J-4; Augustus F. Hawkins, "The Appropriate Remedies for the Deteriorating U.S. Economy," *Congressional Record,* vol. 126 (August 22, 1980), p. E 3971. Lane Kirkland, president of the AFL-CIO, opposes an across-the-board tax cut, as this would deprive the government of moneys to fund social programs, and he favors job-creation programs to benefits that may "trickle down" to labor as a result of tax cuts. "Tax Cuts: Across-the-Board Cuts No Substitute for Jobs Program," *BNA DER,* July 2, 1980, p. G-1; CBO, *An Analysis of the Kemp-Roth Tax Cut Proposal,* pp. 14–17.

[74] Michael Boskin, "Taxation, Saving, and the Rate of Interest," *Journal of Political Economy,* vol. 86 (April 1978), pp. S 3, S 16; GAO, *An Analytical Framework,* pp. 32, 42; and see John Beck, "An Analysis of the Supply-Side Effects of Tax Cuts in an IS-LM Model," *National Tax Journal,* vol. 32 (December 1979), pp. 497–98.

[75] *Congressional Record,* vol. 126 (August 18, 1980), p. S 11153.

[76] GAO, *An Analytical Framework,* pp. 1–2, 9; Richard W. Rahn, "U.S. Relies on Easing Tax Burden," *Washington Star,* November 9, 1980, p. B-1; Toby Roth, "Tax Reduction and Job Creation Act," *Congressional Record,* vol. 126 (July 25, 1980), pp. E 3609-E 3610; Executive Office of the President, *Economic Report of the President—1979,* pp. 128, 184; Edward F. Denison, *Accounting for United States Economic Growth: 1929–1964* (Washington, D.C.: The Brookings Institution, 1974), p. 139.

[77] "Tax Cuts: Gramley Says Less Spending, Not Lower Taxes, Best Way to Cure Inflation," *BNA DER,* September 19, 1980, p. G-10; "Economic Policy: JEC Report Urges $25 Billion Supply Side Tax Cut," p. LL-1.

[78] "Brookings Calls '70s 'The Most Disappointing,'" pp. D-1–D-2; "Economic Policy: Brookings Papers Attack Supply-Side Rationale for Tax Reductions," p. L-4; Senate and House Committees on the Budget, *The Economic Outlook at Midyear 1980,* p. xvii. The latter report states that tax policy to increase growth in productivity is likely to be more successful if tax incentives are concentrated in the industrial sector as opposed to the commercial or residential sectors.

[79] Barry Bosworth, "Tax Policy and Economic Growth," in *National Journal Issues Book* (Washington, D.C.: National Journal, 1977), p. 17.

[80] Denison, *Accounting for United States Economic Growth,* p. 139.

[81] House Report 96-732, p. 4; "Senate Finance Committee Report on H.R. 5829 'Tax Reduction Act of 1980,'" *BNA DER,* September 18, 1980, p. 32.

82 "Economic Outlook: Chamber of Commerce Attacks Administration Economic Program," p. LL-1 (statement of Rahn); Kemp, "What Does President Carter Have Against the U.S. Economy?" p. H 8128; "Joint Committee on Taxation Staff's Explanation of '2-4-7-10' Depreciation Proposal," *BNA DER*, August 21, 1980, p. J-1; "Senate Finance Committee Report on H.R. 5829, 'Tax Reduction Act of 1980,'" p. 32 (additional views of seven Republican senators); "Small Business: Tax Burden Concern High," *BNA DER*, October 10, 1980, pp. K-1, K-3; "Economic Policy: Reagan Unveils 5-Part Revitalization Plan," *BNA DER*, September 9, 1980, pp. LL-6, LL-9 (remarks of Conable).

83 Clarence J. Brown, "Tax Issues Must Be Addressed," *Congressional Record*, vol. 126 (October 2, 1980), p. E 4769. Since the administration would limit the maximum benefit from depreciation and the investment tax credit to no more than the benefit of expensing, critics fear that Treasury regulations may set a discount rate for calculating expensing that will be less favorable than they would like.

84 Martin Feldstein, "Tax Incentives without Deficits," *Congressional Record*, vol. 126 (July 31, 1980), p. S 10475. GAO agrees that lowering "risk premiums" and correcting for inflation-induced distortions through partial indexing of the tax system would contribute to increased capital formation. General Accounting Office, *An Analytical Framework*, p. 79.

85 House Report 96-732, p. 11. Economists Dale W. Jorgenson and Alan J. Auerbach of Harvard University also recommend allowing businesses to depreciate fully the present discounted value of capital assets in the year that the assets are acquired. Dale Tate, "Political Campaigns Draw Battle Lines over Tax Cuts," *Congressional Quarterly*, vol. 38 (August 2, 1980), pp. 2155, 2157. The president of the National Coal Association argues that business should have the option to expense the cost of government-mandated nonproductive equipment in the year of purchase. *Hearings on Advisability of a Tax Cut*, August 31, 1980, statement of Bagge, p. 30. Bagge also points out that some mining equipment such as bulldozers and graders is now depreciable in less than five years because it is used twenty-four hours a day. He recommends the option of faster depreciation than that allowed for such equipment under the 10-5-3 plan. Ibid., pp. 4–5.

86 Martin Feldstein, *Adjusting Depreciation in an Inflationary Economy: Indexing versus Acceleration*, National Bureau of Economic Research, October 2, 1979. Feldstein assumes that ADR was intended as an investment incentive and not as a device to offset the effects of inflation. For other estimates of the effect of the 10-5-3 depreciation reform in offsetting the effects of inflation, see *The Capital Cost Recovery Act Proposal*, pp. 8–13.

87 *Hearings on Capital Cost Recovery*, October 22, 1979, statement of Robert S. McIntyre, pp. 2–3. McIntyre assumes a $110 equipment cost with a $10 salvage value, 10 percent inflation and a 46 percent tax rate. He also assumes a half-year convention and used a nominal discount rate of 15 percent.

88 "Economic Policy: Carter's Industrial Program Not Cure-all for Economy," *BNA DER*, September 5, 1980, pp. K-1–K-2; "Tax Cuts: Finance Oks Individual Cuts, Bentsen Depreciation Proposal," *BNA DER*, August 20, 1980, pp. G-5, G-7.

89 Jane G. Gravelle, *The Capital Cost Recovery System and the Corporate Income Tax*, Congressional Research Service, September 21, 1979, p. 4, graph 1. Gravelle assumes that assets earn an after-tax return of 4.7 percent and that inflation is 7 percent. *Economic Change Hearings*, pp. 76–82, statement of Professor George F. Break.

90 Gravelle, *The Capital Cost Recovery System,* p. 9.

91 Feldstein, *Adjusting Depreciation in an Inflationary Economy.*

92 *Hearings on Capital Cost Recovery,* statement of G. William Miller, secretary of the Treasury, p. 12. For additional discussion of the effect of the 10-5-3 depreciation reform plan on resource allocation, see *The Capital Cost Recovery Act Proposal,* pp. 19–22.

93 *Congressional Record,* vol. 126 (August 1, 1980), pp. H 7019–H 7020; "The Huge Stakes in 10-5-3 Depreciation," *Business Week,* October 1, 1979, p. 124.

94 "The Huge Stakes in 10-5-3 Depreciation," p. 129.

95 *Hearings on Capital Cost Recovery,* p. 21, statement of Strichman quoting Blumenthal.

96 "Senate Finance Committee Report on H.R. 5829, 'Tax Reduction Act of 1980,'" p. J-18. For a discussion of component depreciation, see Committee on Ways and Means, *Real Estate Depreciation,* April 17, 1978 (Committee print prepared by the staff of the Joint Committee on Taxation).

97 "Housing: Changes in Depreciation Approved by Senate Finance Committee Seen Aiding Housing," *BNA DER,* September 3, 1980, pp. G-1–G-2.

98 "Tax Cuts: Gov. Carey Urges Ways and Means Panel to Approve Gradual Tax Cuts," *BNA DER,* September 9, 1980, pp. G-2–G-3; "Remarks by Senator Lloyd Bentsen (D-Tex.) on Introduction of S. 2040," pp. J-1–J-2.

99 "White Paper on President Carter's Economic Renewal Program," *BNA DER,* August 28, 1980, pp. X-1, X-6; "Treasury Department Fact Sheet on Tax Portions of the President's Economic Renewal Program," *BNA DER,* August 29, 1980, pp. J-1–J-2.

100 Edward M. Kennedy, "Tax Reform Issues," *Congressional Record,* vol. 124 (October 9, 1978), pp. S 17862, S 17867-S 17868; "Explanation and Text of Draft Bill to Provide for Investment Tax Credit Refundability," *BNA DER,* November 2, 1979, p. J-1; "Mr. Carter's Latest Plan," *Washington Post,* August 29, 1980, p. A-18; 26 U.S.C. 46(a)(8)(C) (solar and wind energy property credits).

101 "Economic Policy: Reagan Unveils 5-Part Revitalization Plan," p. LL-8 (statement of Representative Conable); Caroline Atkinson, "Carter's Investment Tax Credit Refund Faces Tough Going," *Washington Post,* August 29, 1980, p. E-1; "An Economic Dream in Peril," p. 52; Kemp, "What Does President Carter Have Against the U.S. Economy?" pp. H 8128–H 8129; Roberts, "Carter's Tax Package," pp. S 14155–S 14156.

102 "White Paper on President Carter's Economic Renewal Program," p. X-6; "Treasury Department Fact Sheet on Tax Portions of President's Economic Renewal Program," p. J-2; "Tax Cuts: Governor Carey Urges Ways and Means Panel to Approve Gradual Tax Cuts," p. G-3; "President's Comments on Economy," *Washington Star,* August 29, 1980, p. A-6.

103 See Robert J. Samuelson, "Investment Incentives: Politics May Come First," *Washington Post,* September 16, 1980, pp. E-1, E-3; "The Basics in Trouble," p. 59; Roberts, "Carter's Tax Package," p. S 14156.

104 26 U.S.C. 46. Special provisions apply to numerous assets and circumstances.

105 "Senate Finance Committee Report on H.R. 5829," pp. J-3, J-22; "Remarks of Sen. Lloyd Bentsen (D-Tex.) on Introduction of S. 3040," p. J-3.

[106] "Senate Finance Committee Report on H.R. 5829," pp. J-3, J-25, J-32; "JCT Staff Summary of Adm'n Proposals on Tax Reductions," *BNA DER*, September 4, 1980, pp. J-1, J-2; Christine Russell, "Economy Plan Has Funds for Research," *Washington Star*, August 29, 1980, p. A-6.

[107] *Hearings on Capital Formation*, June 15, 1977, statement of Woodworth, p. 6; House Report 96-732, p. 8.

[108] "Tax Cut Options Prepared by the Subcommittee on Taxes of the Senate Democratic Task Force on the Economy," *BNA DER*, July 23, 1980, pp. J-1, J-4; House Report 96-732, pp. 8–10.

[109] "Senate Finance Committee Report on H.R. 5829," pp. J-3, J-28–J-29; Symms, "The Venture and Equity Capital Revitalization Act of 1980," pp. E 3977-E 3978; John Edward Porter, "Capital Investment Tax Incentive Act of 1980," *Congressional Record*, vol. 126 (August 27, 1980), pp. E 4077–E 4078; GAO, *An Analytical Framework*, p. 56; "Capital Gains: Securities Industry Pushes for Further Reductions in Tax," pp. K-1, K-3.

[110] "Senate Finance Committee Report on H.R. 5829," pp. J-3, J-11, J-33; "Tax Cuts: Miller Says Carter Still Prefers Postponing Tax Debate Until After Election," *BNA DER*, July 10, 1980, pp. G-6–G-7; *Hearings on Capital Formation*, June 15, 1977, statement of Woodworth, p. 6; GAO, *An Analytical Framework*, pp. 57, 61; Hobart Rowen, "Arthur Burns Hits Tax Cut Now," *Washington Post*, July 9, 1980, p. E-3. Additional changes proposed include the following: The administration's plan calls for making new business start-up costs deductible over a period of not less than sixty months. Currently such costs are not deductible and are only recoverable when the business is sold or terminated. The argument against their deductibility is that these are not expenses incurred in carrying on a trade or business and they should not be depreciated or amortized because no ascertainable useful life can be established for these costs. The administration now favors amortization to reduce controversy and litigation under the present law and to encourage the formation of new businesses. "Treasury Department Fact Sheet on Tax Portions of President's Economic Renewal Program," p. J-4; "JCT Staff Summary of Adm'n Proposals on Tax Reductions," p. J-2. The Senate Finance Committee bill does not contain this reform but it would make various changes in the treatment of progress payments for construction projects for the purpose of the investment tax credit, and the taxpayer could elect to commence depreciation of progress expenditures for taxable years during the construction period rather than wait until the property is placed in use. "Senate Finance Committee Report on H.R. 5829," p. J-20. The Senate Finance Committee bill would increase from $150,000 to $250,000 the minimum accumulated earnings credit that is excluded in calculating the tax on retained earning in excess of the reasonable needs of the corporation. Retained earnings beyond the reasonable needs of the corporation are taxable on the premise that these earnings were retained by the corporation rather than paid out in dividends to help the corporation's shareholders avoid individual income taxes. The Senate Finance Committee would raise the credit—except for certain service corporations that do not need to accumulate as much for their reasonable needs—to adjust for increased costs and to reduce borrowing pressures on small businesses. Ibid., p. J-21. The Finance Committee believes that greater worker productivity is encouraged by employee stock ownership. The committee bill would encourage labor-intensive employers to establish tax-exempt trusts called employee stock ownership plans (ESOPs) by allowing the tax credit for contributions to such plans to be based on employee payrolls as an alternative to the current credit based on stock contributions to the ESOP. Capital-intensive firms are

more likely to take advantage of the credit under current law, whereas labor-intensive firms may have only a small amount of qualified investment and thus are not influenced by the current tax credit to establish ESOPs. Ibid., pp. J-3, J-25.

[111] "JCT Staff Summary of Adm'n Proposals on Tax Reduction," p. J-1; "Treasury Department Fact Sheet on Tax Portions of President's Economic Renewal Program," p. J-2; "Political Campaigns Draw Battle Lines over Tax Cuts," p. 2156; Congressional Budget Office, *An Analysis of the Roth-Kemp Tax Cut Proposal*, 1978, p. 31.

[112] Bill Bradley, "S. 2920—Tax Credit for Social Security Payments," *Congressional Record*, vol. 126 (July 2, 1980), p. S 9194; Caroline Atkinson, "Carter Plan, in Effect, Ties Income Tax into Social Security," *Washington Post*, August 30, 1980, p. A-8; Henry S. Reuss, "We Should Repeal the 1981–82 Payroll Increases Now," *Congressional Record*, vol. 126 (August 27, 1980), pp. H 8023–H 8024; and see Joseph A. Pechman and Benjamin A. Okner, *Who Bears the Tax Burdens?* (Washington, D.C.: The Brookings Institution, 1974), pp. 59-61; Browning and Johnson, *The Distribution of the Tax Burden*, pp. 51–52.

[113] "Tax Plan Favors Business Incentives," *Washington Post*, August 29, 1980, pp. A-1, A-9 (statement of Eizenstat); Representative Richard A. Gephardt, Press Release, June 27, 1980, p. 2; H. Wendel, *Aggregate Economic Effects of Changes in Social Security Taxes*, CBO Technical Paper, August 1978. Estimates of the effect of the increase in the employers' share of social security payroll taxes range from passing back the full amount of the offset in lower wages to passing the full amount of the increase forward to consumers in higher prices. For the first view see, among others, John B. Hagens and John C. Hambor, "The Macroeconomic Effects of a Payroll Tax Rollback," *Eastern Economic Journal*, vol. 6 (January 1980), pp. 21–32. For the second view, see D. Hamermesh, "New Estimates of the Incidence of the Payroll Tax," *Southern Economic Journal*, vol. 45 (April 1979), pp. 1218–19. Representative Gephardt's bill is H.R. 7046; Senator Bradley's bill is S. 2920.

[114] Gephardt, Press Release, p. 1; Richard A. Gephardt, "The Social Security Solution," *Congressional Record*, vol. 126 (August 28, 1980), p. H 8116; table 6 this volume; Bradley, "S. 2920—Tax Credit for Social Security Payments," p. S 9194.

[115] Penner, "The Future Growth of Government Budgets," p. 110.

[116] See, for instance, Richard Musgrave and Peggy Musgrave, *Public Finance in Theory and Practice*, 2nd ed. (New York: McGraw-Hill, 1976), pp. 393, 413; Colin D. Campbell, *The 1977 Amendments to the Social Security Act* (Washington, D.C.: American Enterprise Institute, 1978), p. 4; Atkinson, "Carter Plan, in Effect, Ties Income Tax into Social Security," p. A-8. Representative Gephardt and Senator Bradley would make their tax credit refundable to "benefit those at the very lowest income levels." Bradley, "S. 2920—Tax Credit for Social Security Payments," p. S 9194. If the social security tax is regarded as regressive, some maintain this regressivity is offset by the progressivity of social security benefits as low-income workers receive twice as much in benefits per dollar contributed as do higher-income wage earners.

[117] "Economic Policy: Fed Chairman Opposes Both Carter and Reagan Tax-Cut Plans," p. LL-1; "Pensions: Social Security Attitude Survey Given to President's Pension Policy Commission," *BNA DER*, October 8, 1980, p. G-1; Spencer Rich, "Social Security Tax Bite Higher in Other Nations," *Washington Post*, July 26, 1980, p. A-5.

[118] See "Tax Cut Options Prepared by the Subcommittee on Taxes of the Senate Democratic Task Force on the Economy," p. J-1 as to the argument that substituting labor for capital discourages capital formation and an increased rate of productivity.

[119] Jonathan Fuerbringer, "Labor Urges No Tax Cut," *Washington Star*, July 29, 1980, p. D-7; Art Pine, "The Tax-Cut Proposal," *Washington Post*, July 6, 1980, p. F-1; Nancy L. Ross, "Anderson Flails GOP Tax Cut," *Washington Post*, July 21, 1980, p. 3, business section; Dale Tate, "Carter Economic Plan: A Timely Melange," *Congressional Quarterly*, vol. 38 (August 30, 1980) p. 2563. Some economists argue that the proper procedure to give general relief is to widen the tax brackets instead of decreasing tax rates. The zero bracket amount, they say, should be increased and exemptions and deductions should be greater as well. The points at which tax rates increase should be farther apart than they now are. If this were done, they argue, the income tax would be more "progressive." Thus, a taxpayer whose income is just high enough to place him in the lowest bracket at a 14 percent rate would be taxed at a 12 percent rate under the Republican proposal. If the tax brackets were widened and the zero bracket amount were raised, however, this person would pay no tax at all. At the other end of the income spectrum, a very wealthy taxpayer would be in the 70 percent bracket whether or not the tax brackets were widened.

[120] Edward F. Denison, "A Note on Private Saving," *Review of Economics and Statistics*, vol. 40 (August 1958), pp. 261–67. For labor response see George F. Break, "Income Taxes and Incentives to Work," *American Economic Review*, vol. 47 (1957), pp. 529-49.

[121] "'Supply-Side' Tax Cuts," *Minneapolis Tribune*, editorial, July 15, 1980.

[122] "Tax Cuts: The Roth-Kemp Bill and the Laffer Curve," *BNA DER*, June 28, 1978, pp. Y-1–Y-3 (statement of Walter W. Heller, professor of economics, University of Minnesota).

[123] U.S. Congress, Joint Economic Committee and Senate Budget Committee, *Hearings on Tax Cut Legislation*, 96th Congress, 2d session, July 23, 1980, statement of Schultze, p. 23.

[124] "Statement of Treasury Secretary G. William Miller Before the Ways and Means Committee," *BNA DER*, July 22, 1980, pp. J-1, J-4.

[125] Rowland Evans and Robert Novak, "The Tax Cut Trap," *Washington Post*, July 25, 1980, p. A-13.

[126] "Economic Policy: Carter Unveils New Stimulus Package," *BNA DER*, August 28, 1980, pp. LL-1, LL-4; "Middle-Income Americans Pay 60.1 Percent of Taxes," *Washington Post*, September 13, 1980, p. A-7; "No Free Lunch," *Richmond News Leader*, editorial, July 9, 1980; "Tax Returns: Top 10% of Earners Paid Half of $188.6 Billion in Individual Income Taxes," *BNA DER*, July 17, 1980, p. G-1; "Tax Cuts: Witnesses Differ over Timing, Scope of Tax Cuts," *BNA DER*, July 24, 1980, pp. G-10, G-11. The Tax Foundation claims that if the federal government should confiscate all earnings now taxed at rates above 50 percent, the additional tax revenues would run the government for only six and three-tenths days. "Tax Rates: Taxing Top Earnings at 100 Percent Would Run U.S. Less than Week," *BNA DER*, September 2, 1980, p. G-2.

[127] Roth, "Reagan-Roth-Kemp," pp. S 14155, S 14156. "Reducing marginal tax rates, for example, would have more impact on incentives than increasing the standard deduction," according to Congressional Budget Office, *The Economic Outlook at Midyear 1980*, p. 59.

[128] Bruce Bartlett, "The Case for Supply-Side Economics," *Policy Report*, vol. 2 (August 1980), pp. 1–5.

¹²⁹ Bethell, "What Kemp-Roth Would Really Do," p. A-17.

¹³⁰ *Congressional Record,* vol. 126 (September 4, 1980), p. S 12095.

¹³¹ Bethell, "What Kemp-Roth Would Really Do," p. A-17.

¹³² U.S. Congress, Senate Committee on the Budget, *Hearings on Leading Economists Views of the Kemp-Roth,* 95th Congress, 2d session, August 1978, (hereafter *Leading Economists*) p. 141, statement of Penner.

¹³³ *Leading Economists,* Letter from Paul W. McCracken, pp. 121–22.

¹³⁴ See Herbert Stein, "My Case for Reagan," *Wall Street Journal,* September 10, 1980, p. 26.

¹³⁵ Boris I. Bittker, "Federal Income Taxation and the Family," *Stanford Law Review,* vol. 27 (July 1975), p. 1428.

¹³⁶ See H.R. 3609 by Representative Millicent Fenwick (R-N.J.) and S. 339 by Senator Charles McC. Mathias, Jr. (R-Md.). The Fenwick bill has more than 240 sponsors and at least 100 members of the House have signed a discharge petition to secure early House consideration. See "Tax Legislation: Rep. Fenwick's Petition to Bring 'Marriage Tax' Bill to House Floor Gaining Support," *BNA DER,* October 9, 1980, p. G-1, and "Tax Legislation: Finance Subcommittee Sets Aug. 5 Hearings on 'Marriage Penalty' Proposals," *BNA DER,* July 24, 1980, p. G-1, citing still other bills introduced to deal with the marriage penalty. If married couples were allowed to file as if they were single, couples with the same total incomes but different distributions of income would in some cases pay different amounts of taxes. "Senate Finance Committee Report on H.R. 5829," p. J-10. For example, suppose tax rates were 10 percent up to $20,800 and 15 percent thereafter. A couple with taxable incomes of $15,000 for each spouse would pay a total tax of $3,000 (1,500 + 1,500), assuming there is no zero bracket amount. But a couple with the same total income of $30,000 distributed in the sum of $25,000 to one spouse and $5,000 to the other would pay a tax of $4,250 (3,750 + 500). Thus, reduction of the marriage tax would still leave a difference in taxes from couple to couple. The Senate Finance Committee contends its proposal is simpler than the Fenwick-Mathias plan, since it would not require couples to calculate their taxes under two alternatives to decide which alternative saves more in taxes. Ibid. Also, the Fenwick-Mathias approach, it is claimed, would require new and possibly complicated rules relating to the division of income, exemptions, deductions, and credits between the spouses. And finally, the deduction approach would result in a lower revenue loss to the Treasury than the Fenwick-Mathias approach.

¹³⁷ Millicent Fenwick, "Taxes Are Punishing the Working Couple," *Philadelphia Bulletin,* April 14, 1980.

¹³⁸ *Congressional Record,* vol. 125 (April 10, 1979), p. E 1711.

¹³⁹ "Administration Still Has No Recommendations to Ease Marriage 'Penalty,'" *BNA DER,* August 5, 1980, pp. G-3–G-4.

¹⁴⁰ Robert J. Samuelson, "Congress' Bag of Tax Cut Proposals," *National Journal,* June 21, 1980, p. 1007.

¹⁴¹ "Sin Tax," *Washington Post,* editorial, July 24, 1979.

¹⁴² The administration's welfare reform proposal, if adopted, would increase the EITC to 12 percent of the first $5,000 in income for a new maximum of $600, but the credit

would not be available to families of wage earners holding public service employment funded in whole or in part under the Comprehensive Employment and Training Act. Denial of the credit to these families would be used to encourage those holding public service jobs to seek jobs in the private sector. The welfare reform proposal, if adopted, would increase the average credit from $310 per family to $375. *The Administration's 1979 Welfare Reform Proposal,* American Enterprise Institute Legislative Analysis, no. 7 (Washington, D.C., 1979), pp. 8–9, 29.

[143] "Senate Finance Committee Report on H.R. 5829," p. J-10; "Treasury Department Fact Sheet on Tax Portions of President's Economic Renewal Program," p. J-2. The current EITC more than offsets the wage earner's share of social security payroll taxes and the payroll taxes of the self-employed who are eligible. If the employer's share of the payroll is shifted back to wage earners, as some contend, the EITC does not fully offset workers' payroll taxes. See Colin D. Campbell and William L. Peirce, *The Earned Income Credit* (Washington, D.C.: American Enterprise Institute, 1980), table 7, p. 21.

[144] Campbell and Peirce, *The Earned Income Credit,* pp. 9-10.

[145] Joseph A. Pechman, *Federal Tax Policy,* 3rd ed. (Washington, D.C.: The Brookings Institution, 1977), p. 102.

[146] *The Administration's 1979 Welfare Reform Proposal,* p. 27.

[147] See Martin Anderson, "The Roller Coaster Income Tax," *Public Interest,* no. 50 (Winter 1978), pp. 19-25.

[148] Calculated from U.S. Department of the Treasury, Internal Revenue Service, *Individual Income Tax Returns, Statistics of Income 1977,* Publication 78 (6-80), p. 118. Note that these statistics were compiled before the 1978 EITC reforms which changed the credit and phase-out ranges. This conclusion should not be changed by the reforms, however.

[149] Campbell and Peirce, *The Earned Income Credit,* pp. 9–14.

[150] Robert Ball, *Social Security Today and Tomorrow* (New York: Columbia University Press, 1978), pp. 430–31; Alicia H. Munnell, "The Social Security System: An Overview," in Michael J. Boskin, ed., *The Crisis in Social Security* (San Francisco: Institute for Contemporary Studies, 1977), pp. 92–93.

American Enterprise Institute for Public Policy Research
1150 Seventeenth Street, N.W.   Washington, D.C. 20036   (202) 862-5800